Contents

 KW-443-492

Introduction for students
Introduction for teachers

Section 4   The threatening universe

Section 5   One great step . . .

Section 6   The big idea: Charles Darwin

A NEW WINDMILL BOOK OF THE NATURAL WORLD

Stranger than Fiction

Edited by John O'Connor

Heinemann
New Windmills

Heinemann Educational Publishers
Halley Court, Jordan Hill, Oxford OX2 8EJ
A division of Reed Educational & Professional Publishing Ltd

OXFORD   MELBOURNE   AUCKLAND
JOHANNESBURG   BLANTYRE   GABORONE
IBADAN   PORTSMOUTH (NH) USA   CHICAGO

Selection, introduction and activities © John O'Connor, 2001
Literacy adviser: Lynn Lawes

04 03 02 01
10 9 8 7 6 5 4 3 2 1

ISBN 0 435 12533 8

The publishers gratefully acknowledge the following for permission to reproduce
copyright material. Every effort has been made to trace copyright holders, but in some
cases this has proved impossible. The publishers would be happy to hear from any
copyright holder that has not been acknowledged.

BBC Worldwide for *Lifesense* by John Downer, © John Downer, 1991; *Walking With
Dinosaurs* by Tim Haines, © Tim Haines, 1999; reproduced by permission of BBC
Worldwide Ltd. John Brown Publishers for 'It's raining sprats and cods', 'Plummeting
cows', 'Baffling biology' and 'Big shot', which appeared on the *Fortean Times* website:
www.forteantimes.com; reproduced by permission of the publisher. Channel Four for
Alexander Graham Bell by Moorcroft and Magnusson; reproduced by permission of
Channel Four Television. Domino Books for *The Private Life of Plants* by David
Attenborough, BBC Books, 1995. Faber & Faber Ltd for *The Unnatural Nature of
Science* by Lewis Wolpert, published by Faber & Faber Ltd, 1992. HarperCollins
Publishers for *Life on Earth* and *The Trials of Life* by David Attenborough, published by
HarperCollins Ltd. Lee Krystek for 'Explaining the Inexplicable' and 'Ten Arms and an
Eye' from the website of The Unmuseum: www.unmseum.mus.pa.us Little Brown for
'Floating Fire' from *Weird Weather* by Paul Simons, published by Little Brown & Co,
1996. *Reader's Digest* for *Sharks: Silent Hunters of the Deep,* published by Reader's
Digest, 1986 and *Life on Earth* by David Attenborough, published with HarperCollins,
1979; 'Voyage of discovery' from *Darwin and the Beagle* by Alan Moorehead,
reproduced by permission of Laurence Pollinger Ltd and the Estate of Alan Moorehead.

Illustrations by Jackie Hill at 320 Design: 'It's raining sprats and cods' – John Holder;
'Plummeting cows' – Julian Mosedale; 'Clash of the titans' – Alan Baker; 'The night the
stars fell' – Hashim Akib; 'The giant tortoise' – Alan Baker.

Photos: Venus's flytrap – NHPA/ANT; dolphins – FLPA/Gerard Lacz; Portuguese man-o'-war
– Bruce Coleman Collection; rattlesnakes – BBC Natural History Unit/Rupert Barrington;
Wright brothers' first flight – Mary Evans Picture Library; Charles Darwin – NHPA.

Cover design by PCP Design Consultancy
Typeset by ᴛA Tek-Art, Croydon, Surrey
Cover photo by Rex Features
Printed and bound in the United Kingdom by Clays Ltd, St Ives plc

Introduction for students

The extracts in this book all come under the heading of 'science writing'. But that can cover anything from the 'weird science' of UFOs and mysterious floating fireballs, to a description of the giant squid or an account of what happens if an asteroid hits the Earth.

Some of the writers are famous people such as Charles Darwin or David Attenborough. Others, like the reporters for the spooky *Fortean Times*, are simply people who have experienced something strange and want to share it with others.

The activities at the end of each section are to help you understand the extracts a little better and find new ways of looking at them. By the end you should have some idea of what makes really good science writing.

I hope you will enjoy reading these extracts. You can start off with an amazing story about a shower of fish, lose some sleep reading about the things that inhabit our beds, and end by learning about one of the greatest scientists who has ever lived. In between, you will share some strange and powerful experiences – I hope they give you the inspiration to write about your own.

John O'Connor

Introduction for teachers

The revised National Curriculum for English includes the requirement for students to engage with a range of 'non-fiction and non-literary texts'. The National Curriculum divides this category into four areas, one of which is writing about the natural world. *Stranger than Fiction* has been designed to meet the needs of this requirement.

The extracts included in this collection have been carefully selected to interest and motivate Key Stage 3 students. The extracts have been arranged thematically. Students can begin by enjoying some of the more bizarre aspects of science before moving on to compare the different ways in which science writers have written about the world of predators or expressed their awe at the power of the universe. The concluding section offers the opportunity to follow the career of a great scientist in a variety of styles and formats, including his own writing.

Following each themed section is a range of activities tailored to explore each extract in line with the demands of the proposed Framework for Teaching English at Key Stage 3. There are also activities that allow for comparative work across a selection of extracts. Support for the language-based activities can be found on the website: www.newwindmills.co.uk/strangerthanfiction/support

Care has been taken to build in differentiation within each section. This is provided through the subject matter (from exploding melons to Darwin's journals); the varying difficulty of language (from tabloid newspapers to scientific explanation); and in the activities themselves.

I hope you will find that *Stranger than Fiction* is a valuable resource in helping to meet the non-fiction requirements for all your Key Stage 3 students.

John O'Connor

Section 1
Weird science

There are some things in the world around us which are almost impossible to believe. Yet people have seen them and recorded their experiences. In this section you will read about fish which fall from the sky like rain; balls of light that float around the house; and cows which are reported to have crashed onto the decks of boats in the middle of the ocean. It's all stranger than fiction.

It's raining sprats and cods
Fortean Times

Imagine that you are walking through the countryside and it suddenly starts to rain. There's nothing unusual in that – except that this time the rain-drops are fish! Don't be too shocked. In Australia alone there have been over seventy reported fish-falls in the last 120 years. Here are some of them, starting with the story of a priest in Sydney, who was outside his church one day when a live, wriggling fish fell out of the sky and landed on his shoulder.

The fish hit him as he was hurrying across the courtyard of his North Sydney presbytery in a torrential downpour one day in March 1966. Reacting quickly, he caught the fish as it slid down his chest and looked around to see who might have thrown it – there was not a soul in sight. Just then the creature slipped from his grasp, splashed

onto the flooded ground and swam away leaving the dazed **divine** standing there, soaked and stunned.

Sceptics might suggest that the priest had been at the altar wine, but fortunately for the good father his claim is supported by hundreds of similar reports from many parts of the world – and by dozens of such stories from Australia.

On 6 February 1989, for instance, Harold and Debra Degen stared in disbelief as hundreds of sardine-sized fish cascaded onto their home in Rosewood, near Ipswich, Queensland.

While working in his yard at about 11:30am Mr Degen heard what sounded like hail, turned around and was amazed to see the ground covered with hundreds of little fish. The last few fell as he watched. Debra's first thought was that her husband was playing a joke. 'But when I looked around my front lawn they were everywhere. It was very frightening,' she said.

Rosewood is situated on a tributary of the Brisbane River but is about 38 miles (60km) – as the fish flies – from the sea.

---

divine: priest
sceptics: people who do not believe in something

The Degens collected almost 800 fish, all of which were dead, their bellies burst and cold to the touch. Some were 'clumped' or stuck together. They fell only on the Degens' property and the road outside, and were confined to a strip about 87×20ft (27×6m). All of them were bream.

No planes or cars were evident and Harold insisted he could not have been hoaxed: 'I was really stunned. I hope it happens again.'

Raining fish
John Downer

John Downer has made a study of strange phenomena like this. As he admits here, although we *think* we know what causes fish to rain from the sky, no-one has come up with a truly reliable explanation.

Reports of fish raining from the sky hover on the thin boundary between the unexplained and the limits of present knowledge. Such tales date back to the era of the ancient Greeks, but the **phenomenon** is far from mythological – in this century there have been hundreds of well-documented reports. Sixty have come from Australia alone, and Britain, India, the USA and parts of Africa have all experienced fishy downpours.

The details vary. Sometimes the fish tumble while still alive, flapping helplessly on the ground as though just splashed out of some **celestial** lake, sometimes they plummet dead or frozen, as if discarded from an orbiting supermarket freezer. To add to the confusion they may descend in a mixture of the different states, and falls may involve anything from a single fish to cascading shoals of several hundred.

Fish that fall singly or in small numbers are the easiest to understand – birds have probably dropped them. Fish-eating birds carry their catches in their crop or their talons and this makes them easy targets for scavengers, which dive down and **harry** them. In this

phenomenon: strange happening
celestial: heavenly

aerial dogfight the victim will often shed its load to help its escape, giving the **marauder** an easy meal. Such confrontations are surprisingly common; several birds, including skuas and frigate birds, make a living from this kind of piracy. If they fail to catch the **regurgitated** fish it would appear to an observer that it must have fallen from the sky.

Tumbling shoals of fish are less easily explained, but the hidden power of the wind may provide the answer. Tornadoes are among the most studied of all weather phenomena, but their unpredictable nature has helped them remain an **elusive** and mysterious subject. However, studies have revealed a great deal about their enormous power.

Although tornadoes are relatively slow-moving, air within their core churns around at over 500 kilometres an hour. Tremendous drops in air pressure create such huge suction that natural laws appear to be turned upside down. Fragile wheat stems are converted into lethal darts capable of penetrating tree trunks as though fired by some cosmic blowgun. Wooden shards from buildings, sliced and shattered in the spinning vortex, become air-powered missiles that can pierce solid iron.

A tornado also has awesome lifting power – it can rip houses from their foundations and spin them like clothes in a drier; it can pluck up cars and trucks like toys and throw them angrily across the countryside. But it is a fickle wind. When enraged, it rips asunder anything it touches, but it also appears capable of tenderness. It can pluck a horse from a field, transport it 3 kilometres and set it down unharmed; like Dorothy in *The Wizard of Oz*,

---

harry: worry, attack
marauder: raider
regurgitated: brought up
elusive: difficult to pin down

people have also survived similar unscheduled flights.

A wind capable of carrying people and livestock must also have the power to carry and disgorge fish. But if tornadoes are the answer to raining fish, why are they so rarely mentioned by observers?

Tornadoes are the kings of wind, but there are other lesser varieties, such as whirlwinds and dust devils, that can creep by unnoticed but still summon surprising lifting power. It may be that these smaller rotating winds have given rise to the phenomena known as corn circles. Circular impressions in the crop have been reported for hundreds of years and have recently been attributed to the landing marks of alien craft. Hoaxers have now admitted creating the more elaborate modern designs.

When they pass over water, strong winds show another power – they suck the water up into a rotating aquatic column known as a waterspout. Any fish at the surface would be drawn upwards in this liquid conveyor until they reached the angry interior of a storm cloud. **Buoyed up** inside the tormented clouds they could be transported huge distances. By the time the raging forces had calmed down, the fish would be **disgorged** far from their original homes. The fact that many fish-falls feature frozen fish and are often accompanied by hail is consistent with a brief **sojourn** inside a storm cloud.

---

buoyed up: lifted up
disgorged: unloaded
sojourn: stay

Plummeting cows
Daily Mirror

Here is an even stranger story of curious objects falling out of the sky: not fish this time – but a herd of cows! This fictional account appeared to be true when it was published in a daily newspaper.

A Japanese fishing boat had been sunk by a falling cow in the Sea of Okhotsk off the Eastern coast of Siberia. The shipwrecked crew were plucked from the sea, claiming that cows had fallen from the sky and one of them had gone straight through the deck and hull, capsizing the vessel.

The fishermen were arrested for suspected **marine insurance fraud**, but freed after Russian and Japanese investigators found out that the story was true. Russian soldiers based on the island of Sakhalin had used an army transport plane to rustle a herd of cattle. Once airborne, the cattle moved about the aircraft, throwing it off balance. To avoid crashing, the crew drove them out of the large loading bay at the tail of the aircraft at 20,000 ft (6,000m).

---

marine insurance fraud: falsely claiming that there has been an accident at sea, in order to get money out of the insurance company

Floating fire
Paul Simons

For thousands of years there have been reports in all parts of the world of mysterious glowing balls of light which hover in the air or move in and out of buildings. Varying from the size of a golf ball to a football, these strange lights have still not been fully explained. In this extract we read about some frightening experiences.

One June evening in Norwich several years ago, Ron Moore had just returned home from a walk with his wife, Stella, and son, Stephen. The sun was shining, and only the distant rumble of thunder broke the air. Stella went into the kitchen, Stephen to his bedroom at the front of the house, and Ron was just walking down the hall from the garden. Then literally out of the blue came a blinding flash, a huge explosion, and Stephen fell out of his room and lay paralysed on the hall floor.

Stella came out, severely shocked, from the kitchen, paralysed in her hands. Luckily, both her paralysis and Stephen's quickly wore off, but it wasn't until much later that evening that they could talk about what had happened. And the story they told sounds too fantastic the first time you hear it.

Stella had been working at the sink when a glowing ball about the size of a tennis ball floated in through the window, across the kitchen and out the door. It then apparently floated down the hall, before Stephen saw it glide into his bedroom and hover before his eyes, and then he remembered nothing after that.

It all sounds like something out of *Star Trek*. This, and dozens of other accounts of what has become known as ball lightning, have been explained away as hallucinations, or a trick of the eye following a lightning bolt, rather like the flash of a camera going off. But none of these fit the case of the Moore family, simply because their next-door neighbour told them later that he too had seen the ball of light float into their kitchen before the explosion.

Gladys Hughes of Colwyn, North Wales was driving home in her white Fiesta at about 8pm one June evening in 1981 when she ran into a bank of mist rolling off the river on the road between Glan-Conwy and Llanrwst in North Wales. Then she suddenly saw a glowing ball of **translucent** greenish light, about the size of a football, spinning forwards like a wheel with four spikes of light radiating out from it, about a foot away from her side window. Wondering if she'd gone mad or if aliens were visiting from outer space, she slowed down the car, and **in perfect synchrony** so did the ball. She then accelerated and again the ball kept perfect pace. No matter what she did she couldn't shake the thing off, and only when the mist petered out just beyond Dolgarrog Station did the ball suddenly shoot up and away out of sight.

Fearing her sanity was in question, Gladys didn't even plan to mention this back home, but she got an unexpected surprise at the front door. Her husband was waiting there, and told her that he and his golf partner had both seen something fantastic – a glowing green ball shooting up high into the sky, at about 8 p.m.

You could fill a book with the dozens of accounts of ball lightning reported from all over the world.

They have even been seen on board aircraft. This report by the Soviet news agency TASS is of a ball of lightning inside an aircraft on a flight across the former Soviet Union. The ball, 4 inches (10 centimetres) across,

---

translucent: see-through, clear
in perfect synchrony: keeping time perfectly

appeared on the **fuselage** in front of the cockpit of an
Ilyushin-18 aircraft as it few close to a thunderstorm over
the Black Sea on 15 January 1984:

'It disappeared with a deafening noise, but re-emerged
several seconds later in the passenger's lounge, after
piercing in an uncanny way through the air-tight metal
wall,' TASS said. 'The fireball slowly flew above the heads of
the stunned passengers. In the tail section of the airliner it
divided into two glowing crescents which then joined
together again and left the plane almost noiselessly.'

The radar and other instruments aboard the plane
were damaged, and two holes were found in the fuselage,
but no passengers were hurt during the episode.

Of course the **cynics enjoy picking on the credibility
of the witnesses**, but they got a very rude shock several
years ago when no less than a professor of electrical
engineering, Roger Jennison of the University of Kent,
witnessed a glowing ball aboard a plane. It came floating
down the aisle during a Pan Am flight between New York
and Washington, gliding down from the cockpit and
exiting gracefully through the rear toilets.

Another physicist, Arthur Covington, saw one in his
own home and reported it in the science magazine
Nature, 18 April 1970:

'We saw a ball of light emerge from the fireplace and
slowly drift across the room. It appeared to pass through
a curtained, closed window without making any noise or
causing any damage. A loud detonation was heard a few
moments after the ball vanished.'

So what on earth is ball lightning? Physicists,
meteorologists and mathematicians have been locked in

---

fuselage: the main body of an aircraft
cynics enjoy picking on the credibility of the witnesses: some
people laugh and sneer at witnesses who believe they have seen ball
lightning

unseemly warfare on this one for decades. Their explanations range from glowing micro-meteorites to electromagnetic fields of energy that condense into balls of light at their centre.

The phenomenon is clearly electrical. Several electrical workers have witnessed strange glowing balls during their work, often involving high-voltage equipment. For example, there have been reports of overhead pylon cables collapsing in storms, short-circuiting in a blaze of sparks and sometimes **spawning** giant balls of light rolling along the cables.

One recent theory, from Dr Geoffrey Endean at Durham University, concerns a spinning mass of charges in the air contained in a much larger but invisible electric field. With the charges all lined up somewhat like little bar magnets, and energy flowing backwards and forwards between them, a glowing ball of light is formed. Unfortunately, ball lightning is so rare and so difficult to recreate artificially using high-voltage equipment, that we may never be certain what it is.

Yet the sheer volume of evidence does point to one very neat theory, going some way towards an explanation. Mark Stenhoff of the Tornado Research Organisation (TORRO for short) has been compiling detailed reports on ball lightning for years. Nearly all the accounts happen towards the end of a ferocious thunderstorm, or at the very edge of a thunderstorm so far away that the witness is often unaware of it. The balls frequently precede a colossal bolt of lightning, so powerful that the accompanying thunder is deafening. But once this spectacular superbolt has passed, the storm is dead.

Stenhoff's theory goes like this. A thundercloud is basically a huge fluffy battery, with a top side peppered with positive charges and the bottom steeped in

---

spawning: giving birth to

negative charges. Except that, for reasons we don't quite understand, a pocket of positive charges gets stuck amongst the negative charges on the bottom of the cloud. **Unable to discharge until the negatives have shot their bolts** the positive bubble has to wait until the very end of the last act of the thunderstorm to make a positive discharge creating a spectacular flash of lightning, hence the violent thunderbolt. But with the wind in the right direction and all other conditions just right, the positive bubble might start 'leaking' its charges before the final **death throe** of the superbolt. This leakage shows itself as a glowing ball that is attracted to electrical equipment in confined spaces – hence its floating into aircraft and houses.

Whatever the full story, one thing is for sure. The eye-witnesses all agree that ball lightning is like nothing else on earth, and remains the single most spectacular thing they've ever seen in their lives.

---

unable to discharge until the negatives have shot their bolts: the positive charges are unable to release their power until the negative charges have released theirs
death throe: last dying act

Expecting the unexpected
Lewis Wolpert

In our daily lives, it can be a good thing to rely on 'common sense' or 'intuition' – the kind of understanding which doesn't rely upon reasoning, and is sometimes called 'gut-feeling'. But it can easily lead us astray in the world of science, as we see in these examples of things that seem to go against common sense.

Most people not trained in physics have some sort of vague ideas about motion and use these to predict how an object will move. For example, when students are presented with problems requiring them to predict where an object – a bomb, say – will land if dropped from an aircraft, they often get the answer wrong. The correct answer – that the bomb will hit that point on the ground more or less directly below the point at which the aircraft has arrived at the moment of impact – is often rejected. The underlying confusion partly comes from not recognising that the bomb continues to move forward when released and this is not affected by its downwards fall.

This point is made even more dramatically by another example. Imagine being in the centre of a very large flat field. If one bullet is dropped from your hand and another if fired horizontally from a gun at exactly the same time, which will hit the ground first? They will, in fact, hit the ground at the same time, because the bullet's rate of fall is quite independent of its horizontal motion. That the bullet which is fired is travelling horizontally has no effect on how fast it falls under the action of gravity . . .

Science also deals with enormous differences in scale and time compared with everyday experience. Molecules, for example, are so small that it is not easy to imagine them. If someone took a glass of water, each of whose molecules were tagged in some way, went down to the sea, completely emptied the glass, allowed the water to disperse through all the oceans, and then filled the glass from the sea, then almost certainly some of the original water molecules would be found in the glass. What this means is that there are many more molecules in a glass of water than there are glasses of water in the sea. There are also, to give another example, more cells in one finger than there are people in the world . . .

A further example of where **intuition** usually fails, probably because of the scale, is provided by imagining a smooth globe as big as the earth, round whose equator – 25,000 miles long – is a string that just fits. If the length of the string is increased by 36 inches, how far from the surface of the globe will the string stand out? The answer is about 6 inches, and is independent of whether the globe's equator is 25,000 or 25 million miles long.

---

intuition: common sense, or natural instinct

Explaining the inexplicable
Lee Krystek

There are a lot of people who believe that strange phenomena must be caused by aliens or have something to do with the supernatural. But when you start investigating these stories, a much more ordinary explanation usually presents itself. Take The Strange Case of the *Titanic* Mummy . . .

Among the stories surrounding the sinking of the luxury liner *Titanic* in 1912 was a tale about an unlucky mummy. The mummy's curse was as responsible for that accident as the floating island of ice that tore open the ship's hull. Though the story had been around for years, it spread rapidly in the wake of the popularity of the film *Titanic*. The tale goes something like this:

In the late 1890s a rich, young Englishman visiting the **archaeological digs** near Luxor, Egypt, purchased the coffin and mummy of the Princess of Amen-Ra. He arranged for it to be shipped back to his home, but was not there to receive it. He disappeared, never to be found. One of his companions on the trip later died, another lost an arm in an accident and a third lost his fortune in a bank failure.

The coffin reached England and was purchased by a businessman. Three members of the businessman's household were injured in an auto accident and his house caught on fire. Convinced that the mummy was unlucky,

---

archaeological digs: sites where people hope to discover more about cultures of the past through the study of remains

the man donated it to the British Museum. The staff at the museum reported hearing loud banging and crying noises coming from the coffin at night. Things were thrown around the exhibit room without explanation. Finally a watchman died. Then a photographer took a photo of the coffin. When he developed it, the image that appeared was so horrifying that the photographer killed himself.

The museum wanted to get rid of the unlucky mummy, but with its reputation they could not even give it away. Finally, an American archaeologist, who didn't believe in the stories, purchased the mummy and coffin and had it sent back to the States on board the *Titanic*. The rest was, well, history . . .

Another version of this story has the archaeologist bribing the *Titanic* crew to have the mummy put into a life boat and later it winds up in New York City. The mummy is sold and shipped again and involved in one or two more shipwrecks before winding up on the bottom of the sea.

Is this a true story? Or just a weird tale?

Shipping records show no mummy was on board the *Titanic* (this may be why some versions of the tale say that the archaeologist smuggled it aboard). In no account by any *Titanic* survivor do they mention sharing a life boat with a mummy (which wouldn't have been easy to forget). Nor did any rescuer report taking a mummy on board.

The tale probably has its origins with two Englishmen named Douglas Murray and TW Stead. Murray and Stead claimed that an acquaintance of theirs bought a mummy in Egypt and had it placed in a drawing room in his home. The next morning every breakable item in the room had been smashed. The next night the mummy was left in another room with the same results.

The pair also visited the British Museum and saw the

coffin lid of Priestess Amun (there wasn't ever a mummy, only the lid). They decided that the face depicted on it was a tormented horror. Combining the two stories, that of the breakable items and the scary lid, the two sold the tale to the newspapers. The tale later grew to include the *Titanic*.

The *Titanic* portion of the story may have been inspired by the loss of the Menkaure **sarcophagus** in 1838. The sarcophagus, which was being shipped from Egypt to England, was considered to be one of the finest examples of art from the Old Kingdom period. It went to the bottom of the sea when the ship carrying it, the *Beatrice*, sunk in deep water somewhere near Cartagena.

The truth is that the Priestess Amun coffin lid (British Museum item No. 22542) is still sitting quietly in the British Museum's second Egyptian room, where it can be seen today.

---

sarcophagus: a stone coffin, typically associated with ancient Egypt, Rome and Greece

Activities

It's raining sprats and cods

1 News articles can have many purposes: for example to inform, to shock, to criticise, to amaze and to entertain. What do you think is the purpose of this news article? What makes you think this? The language it uses gives you some clues.

2 The headline is a pun to catch the reader's attention. It takes a common saying and replaces two of the words with others that rhyme with the original words. Can you identify the original saying?

3 In what ways does the writer engage the reader's attention in this introduction? Pick out words and phrases that the writer uses to hold the reader's interest and explain their effect.

Word or phrase	Effect
Imagine	appeals directly to the reader and makes them stop and think
Suddenly	implies urgency

4 The article itself is a recount text (a piece of writing where the writer retells events that have happened). Pick out examples of verbs written in the past tense like 'was hurrying' in the first sentence. Rewrite either the story of the priest or the Degens; use the present tense and the first person, as if it is happening to you.

Raining Fish

1 In this extract, the writer uses technical vocabulary such as 'crop', 'talons', 'pressure', 'suction', 'vortex', 'tornadoes'. Try to find out what these terms mean. What effect does the use of terms like these have?

2 Perhaps the most powerful descriptive technique used in this piece is personification. This is when a writer applies

human characteristics to an object or phenomenon.
John Downer does this when he compares the effects of
the tornado to an angry child throwing toys. What do
you think he is trying to achieve by using this technique?

Plummeting cows

1 This is an urban legend. Legends are popular stories that
have been passed down from generation to generation
and are accepted as being at least partly true. In contrast,
an urban legend is a story that has been made up but is
written in a particular way in order to convince the reader
that it really happened. One technique used in urban
legends is the inclusion of lots of facts and figures. Try to
find examples of this technique in the text, for example:

- place names
- testimony from witnesses
- scientific explanations
- details.

2 Write your own urban legend. Try to make it convincing.
Remember that it should contain facts and figures, be
written in the past tense, include technical terms, link
information using temporal connectives e.g. once, then,
when, after and contain testimony from witnesses.

You could start with 'This really happened to a friend of
mine…'

Floating fire

1 In this recount text, the author describes encounters with
ball lightning in different parts of the world. He cleverly
sets the scene in the first paragraph and arouses the
reader's interest. How does he do this?

2 The report uses adjectives and adverbs to build suspense
and tension, for example: 'blinding', 'huge', 'severely',
'quickly'. Try to find other examples in the text. Remember
adjectives describe nouns and adverbs describe verbs.

Adjectives	Adverbs
Glowing	Suddenly

3 The author describes a number of different accounts of sightings of ball lightning in a series of paragraphs. Summarise the key issues in each sighting, using bullet points.

4 Write the script for a television news report on one of these sightings. Include interviews with the witnesses as well as with experts who can explain the phenomenon.

Expecting the unexpected

1 This text attempts to persuade the reader that common sense is often useless when it comes to understanding scientific phenomena. The author uses a variety of techniques to argue his case. They include:

- illustrating points with examples
- exaggeration (overstating the truth) and bias
- addressing the reader directly and writing in the present tense.

2 Pick out at least two examples of each. Having used these techniques, do you think the author achieves his purpose?

Explaining the inexplicable

1 This text begins with an introduction, then describes the events, and ends by explaining the truth behind the story. What do you notice about the use of tenses throughout this piece?

2 The story of the mummy's curse is designed to shock. Which words and phrases does the author use to create this effect? Choose one word or phrase designed to shock and explain how it creates the intended effect. Add a sentence of your own using similar techniques.

3 The author is attempting to make the reader question the truth of the story. How does the author do this?

Comparing the extracts

1 In small groups, look back through each of the examples of weird science in this section and discuss how far you believe that they are scientific fact. Does ball lightning really exist? Can an Egyptian mummy be cursed? When you have discussed each example, give it a mark out of ten (10 = I am sure this is scientific fact; 0 = I am sure this does not really exist, or did not happen). Then add one or two reasons to support each of your judgements. When you have finished your grading, compare it with another group's and talk about any differences.

2 Here is an article on UFOs from an encyclopedia for young readers.

UFOs

The letters 'UFO' are the initials of the words 'unidentified flying object'. A UFO might be anything someone sees in the sky and cannot explain. The kinds of things people claim to see are mysterious lights or 'flying saucers'.

Most sightings can probably be explained quite easily, either as natural things such as clouds or lightning, or as man-made things such as aircraft, satellites or scientific balloons.

Some people believe that UFOs are signs of living visitors from space. Others have deliberately set out to create a hoax by faking photographs and telling lies.

So far, no one has produced evidence that will satisfy the majority of scientists that life exists beyond the Earth.

Write a similar entry of around 100 words for another strange phenomenon, such as crop-circles or the Loch Ness monster. Use the same structure as this entry on UFOs:

- an introductory paragraph which gives an explanation or a definition of the subject
- examples of some of the rational explanations
- other explanations
- a conclusion.

Unnatural nature

You don't have to turn to science fiction if you want to encounter meat-eating plants or animals behaving like humans. The world of nature can supply its own extraordinary stories . . .

Baffling biology
Fortean Times

The *Fortean Times* is a magazine which reports strange phenomena – anything from exploding melons to vampire ants. Here are some short stories reported from different parts of the world.

Booming melons

The American Deep South has been hit by an outbreak of exploding melons – in fields, stores, fridges and kitchens. Tom McElroy of Dadeville, Alabama, took a ten-pounder home and left it in his kitchen.

'Ten minutes later I was dripping in juice and my place looked like a war zone,' he said, after the fruit went off rather more quickly than might be expected. Experts think a bacterial disease is causing gas build-ups inside the melons.

Dolphins to the rescue

François Colombier was out in a 10-foot rubber dinghy with his son and a friend when they were caught in a violent storm, off Brittany in October 1993. Low on fuel and with the outboard motor spluttering, they were tossed about by 10-foot waves.

Suddenly four dolphins appeared. Two took up positions at the stern and one on either side. Then they nudged against the boat and guided it away from nearby rocks. Half an hour later, the dolphins had brought the boat safely to shore, and swam off to sea again.

BEAR-FACED CHEEK

At an airstrip on Alaska's Barter Island, teams of polar bears have taken to walking in a dead straight line to the runway's landing lights, and then bashing them until they go out. Naturalists are mystified.

DANCING TREE

A small tree in Yunnan Province, China, is said to 'dance' to music, the trunk swaying in time with the rhythm and the leaves turning from side to side. When the music ceases, the tree stops moving. Gentle conversation has the same effect, but the tree ignores **raucous** voices and loud **martial** music.

---

raucous: noisy, rowdy
martial: warlike

VAMPIRE ANTS

In March 1993, the town of Envira in the Amazon jungle was invaded by vast swarms of giant blood-drinking ants. The 10,000 residents were forced to wear plastic bags round their ankles, and fought back with poison and boiling water, but to no avail. Seeking meat, salt and blood, the ants devoured cats, chickens and turtles, leaving nothing but the bones behind. Children were at risk, and people who died were buried 40 miles away, as the local graveyard was no longer safe.

The ants appeared after local jungle was cleared, **eliminating** their natural predators, such as birds and spiders.

Within a few weeks they'd conquered 70% of the town, with ant-hills every four yards.

---

eliminating: getting rid of

Big shot
Fortean Times

Bigfoot . . . Abominable Snowman . . . Sasquatch . . . Yeti . . . These are some of the many names given to the strange man-ape sighted by travellers and explorers in different parts of the world. But does it really exist? To find out, there are people planning to shoot one . . .

The debate about whether or not a Bigfoot creature should be shot to help scientists better protect the species is not a new one. The record of sightings of giant hairy man-beasts in North America goes back nearly 200 years and in that time there have been many attempts to shoot one. As many of these sightings were made by seasoned hunters, it is somewhat surprising that no-one has yet produced a dead one – assuming that the creature now called Bigfoot or Sasquatch really does exist.

It seems that many hunters have fired at Bigfoot but it is often too quick for them and they have been unable to hit it. Sometimes, when the hunter's bullets find their mark, the creature has seemed unworried by their impact, even when fired at point-blank range.

In 1914, five men prospecting in Washington's Cascade Mountains claimed to have been attacked by several Bigfoot creatures in a canyon. One of the men said that he fired three shots into one creature's head and two more into its body but it kept running. Gary Joanis was another hunter who fired at a Bigfoot, this one having just stolen the deer he had shot! Joanis and a colleague were hunting at Wanoga Butte in Oregon, in 1957, when the 9ft (2.75m) Bigfoot suddenly appeared, picked up the dead deer and carried it off under its arm. Annoyed, Joanis fired his .306 rifle repeatedly at the beast's back as it departed but it gave no sign that it had been injured . . . unless its 'strange whistling scream' was a cry of pain. It kept on walking and Joanis had no choice but to let it go.

Fourteen-year-old James Lynn Crabtree was equally powerless when he tried to stop a Bigfoot. Out squirrel hunting near his home in Fouke, Arkansas, in 1965, he encountered an 8ft (2.4m) creature which turned to face him and then walk towards him. The boy shot it in the face three times with his shotgun but it showed no sign of hesitating, so he fled.

Two years later, a group of teenagers armed with heavy-calibre weapons hunted several Bigfoot which had been seen around the Dalles in Oregon. One of the hunters saw a 7ft (2.1m) creature in a crouching position and blasted it in the chest with his 12-gauge shotgun. This knocked the creature down and it rolled over twice before it stood up and smashed its way through a fence, snapping off the fence-posts. The hunters returned the next day to follow the tracks and collect the carcass but after 100 yards (90m) they lost the tracks as there were no bloodstains to follow.

Meat-eating plants
David Attenborough

The Venus' flytrap isn't especially rare – many people have them in their homes. But, when you think about what it does and how it works, it is surely one of the most spectacular and extraordinary plants in the whole of the natural world. David Attenborough describes its strange and disturbing method of capturing prey.

Venus's flytrap is related to the sundews, but it is the only species of that family to have evolved such an elaborate trap. It lives only in one small patch of marshy coastal country **straddling** the border between North and South Carolina. It too is a **rosette** a few inches across. It has narrow green leaves that at the end are **prolonged** into two reddish, kidney-shaped **lobes** on either side of the **midrib**. The outer **margin** of each lobe is fringed by a line of spikes and, just beneath them, there is a band of **nectar glands**. The open face of each lobe carries a few isolated bristly hairs. There are usually three, but there may be two, four or, just occasionally, more.

An insect, attracted by the nectar or the red coloration can crawl around on the surface of a lobe **with impunity**,

---

straddling: overlapping
rosette: flat, circle-shaped arrangement of leaves
prolonged: stretched out into
lobes: flat, rounded parts
midrib: central part of the plant
margin: edge
nectar glands: parts of the plant which produce a sweet fluid
with impunity: without getting into trouble

provided it doesn't touch one of these bristles, for they are triggers. Even touching one is not necessarily **lethal**, for nothing will happen immediately. But if it touches the same one or another on the leaf within twenty seconds, then – with a swiftness that may alarm a watching botanist, accustomed as he is to more **sedate** reactions from his subjects – the two lobes snap together. The reaction takes no more than a third of a second. The **stimulus** that triggers it is an electric one but exactly what mechanism drives the closure is, even now, not fully understood.

Although the trap has been sprung, the insect, if it is small, can escape. The spikes on the leaf margins interlock neatly, but not very tightly. A mosquito or an ant can easily crawl out between them. But for larger insects such as a fly, there is no escape. As it thrashes about in its prison, it inevitably touches the triggers again. This stimulates the cells within the lobes to increase rapidly in number, as happens in the bending hairs of a sundew, and the two segments press closer together. They do so with such firmness that the bulge of a fly's body may become visible on the outside. The edges of the lobes form a **hermetic** seal and, within, digestive solutions rich in hydrochloric acid pour from glands on the face of the lobes and start to dissolve the fly's body.

There are two moments during this process when the plant may seem to be less than efficient as a trapper, but both can be interpreted as safety measures that prevent the trap being sprung unnecessarily or uneconomically. Why should the plant require its victim to touch a trigger

---

hermetic: air-tight
lethal: deadly
sedate: calm and slow
stimulus: something that gets a response from something else

hair twice in quick succession? In order that the leaf is not made to close by an **inanimate** object such as a blown leaf falling on to it. And why are the marginal spikes not set closer together? Because an insect below a certain size will not provide enough **sustenance** to compensate for the energy spent in digesting it. If the insect is so small that it does escape, then after twenty minutes or so, the two lobes begin to reopen and twenty-four hours later they are all set to try again.

inanimate: non-living
sustenance: food or fuel

Things that go chomp in the night
John Downer

It isn't a pleasant thought, but you're never alone in bed. As you snuggle up among the sheets and blankets, an army of tiny refuse-collectors sifts and chews its way through your dreams . . . You won't sleep so peacefully after reading this account of dustmites.

Beneath the sheets of even the cleanest bed lurk thousands of eight-legged **scavengers**. Each of us is responsible for sustaining a teeming population that depends on our nightly company for survival. We never notice our uninvited guests because each one is smaller than a speck of dust.

These dustmites are microscopic relatives of spiders and to them the mattress represents the limits of their known world. Many experience their whole lives under a single mattress stud. They are only able to survive in this seemingly barren landscape because each night cells flake from our skin surface and shower down on them like **manna** from heaven.

Every hour 400 million of these skin cells are discarded by each human being, wafting up on the warm air of our bodies and finally settling as part of the dust that covers the furniture of every home. As we undress we create a further blizzard of cells, the greatest quantity ensuing from the electrostatic storm whipped up when tights or socks are removed. As we sleep the skin flakes continue to fall, drifting through the weave of the bedclothes to the dustmites waiting below.

---

scavengers: creatures that live off dead meat and rubbish
manna: the food provided for the Israelites in the Bible

Sustained by this nutritious snowstorm, up to two million dustmites are able to survive in the average mattress. As they graze the vast **savannah** of our sheets, like herds of miniature **wildebeest**, the dustmites attract hunters. Here the diminutive equivalent of lions are a type of predatory mite. These stalk the bed linen, using formidable jaws to pounce on the unsuspecting dustmites and suck them dry.

After **voracious** feeding on our skin and **secretions**, the dustmites **excrete** in quantity. Around 20 pellets of processed skin cells pass through each mite every day. This fine dust adds to the pile of mummified carcasses of dead mites and their cast-off skins that soon accumulate in well-used beds. This debris, tossed into the air by a bed-maker, often induces a fit of sneezing.

The allergic reaction is so severe in some people it can trigger an asthma attack – in fact, the majority of such attacks are believed to be caused by dustmites. Their significance became apparent when European clothes and blankets were taken to Papua New Guinea, where the original tribes have survived until recently with few garments except those made from leaves and grasses. There was an outbreak of asthma as the local inhabitants became exposed to the new organism.

---

sustained: kept alive

savannah: plains in southern Africa

wildebeest: African animals, between an ox and an antelope

voracious: greedy

secretions: substances that the body gives out

excrete: get rid of waste matter from the body

Dolphin doctors
Mark Cawardine

There are many reports of dolphins saving humans from drowning or helping to steer them to land. (You might recall the short account on page 23, for example.) This extract explores a recent theory that dolphins might also have the power to heal.

Research in several countries suggests that dolphins may be able to trigger the healing process in people. It is a claim that has had more than its fair share of **sceptics**, and it is especially difficult to demonstrate scientifically. However, there are so many accounts of dolphins **alleviating cases of chronic depression** or anxiety, **enhancing** recovery from life-threatening illnesses such as cancer, and even speeding up the learning potential of handicapped children, that biologists and doctors around the world are beginning to take it seriously.

Consider some of the evidence. One American study involved two groups of **autistic** children who were believed to be 'beyond hope'. One group was allowed to play with plastic dolphins on a beach, while the other was taken into the water to swim with some real dolphins. The beach children showed no improvement in their condition, but the water children improved dramatically soon afterwards.

---

sceptics: people who do not believe in something
alleviating cases of chronic depression: making people better after they have been depressed for a long time
enhancing: helping
autistic: not able to communicate with others

Other American studies have demonstrated that dolphins can help handicapped children to learn four times more quickly than is possible with other teaching methods, and to **retain** the information for a longer period of time. No one knows exactly how or why, but 'dolphin therapy' is believed to give them more confidence in their own abilities. It is gaining so much respect in the US that some doctors refer handicapped children to dolphin therapy centres, and several health insurance companies will even cover the cost.

Many people suffering from anxiety and depression also seem to benefit from the experience of swimming with dolphins. There is no concrete scientific proof that jumping in the water with them has any long-term benefit, but there are some spectacular examples that provide plenty of intriguing **circumstantial evidence**.

Horace Dobbs, a world-renowned expert on the healing power of dolphins, tells the story of a man who was being treated for chronic depression and had not been able to work for twelve years. Despite the help of specialists, his condition did not improve. In his own words, he was living in 'a black pit of despair'. Then in 1985 Dobbs took the man to swim with Simo, a friendly bottlenose dolphin living near the tiny fishing village of Solva, in Wales. Within moments, the two became inseparable. The man broke his silence and spoke to Simo as if he were talking to an old friend. By the time he had clambered back into the boat, his wife could see traces of the man she had known and loved, and she broke down and cried. For the first time in all those years, the black cloud had started to lift.

There is little doubt that a dolphin can have a powerful effect on human emotions. Few people remain unmoved

---

retain: keep hold of
circumstantial evidence: clues that the theory is right

by a close encounter, especially if they are in the water meeting the dolphin on its own terms. It is an experience that affects everyone in their own way; many report feeling **euphoric** or uplifted, others burst into tears and feel overwhelmed. But either way, it seems to **elicit** an extreme response.

This is particularly interesting because emotions and health of mind play very important roles in the healing process. Good health is more than a mere absence of disease. Contentment, peace of mind, flowing energy and a deep sense of security are all essential ingredients of total well-being.

It has been known for many years that dogs, cats and other animals can play a vital role in maintaining a healthy mind, and healthy body by association. They help anxious people to relax, at least partly because **their affection is unconditional** – it bears no relation to sex, age, size, colour, shape or appearance. Whether dolphin therapy works on exactly the same basis, or whether dolphins have an extra-special quality that we have yet to identify, no one really knows.

Intriguingly, dolphins seem able to recognize depression or illness in people. Researchers have found, time and again, that dolphins have an uncanny ability to home in on the people who most need help, even when there are other people in the water. Again, no one can explain how they are able to do this. One possibility is that, if they are highly sensitive to energy fields, they may be able to pick up **subtle abnormalities** in the fields of

---

euphoric: extremely happy

elicit: bring forth

their affection is unconditional: they love people, regardless of what they are like

subtle abnormalities: very faint signs that something is not working properly

people with health problems. Another is that they can pick up problems with their sophisticated **sonar**, which may enable them to 'see' inside the human body. It may even be psychological: it is often suggested that dolphins are **telepathic** (they certainly seem to be more intuitive than most people), and so they may be able to read minds and emotions.

There are so many unanswered questions (not least of which is a moral one: can we justify this form of dolphin exploitation, as it is seen by some people, for human benefit?). We do not know if the 'dolphin effect' is physical, emotional or spiritual. But even if it is entirely in our own minds, and there is nothing unique about the dolphins themselves, it may yet prove to be a valuable alternative to more conventional treatments. The lack of harmful side-effects, for instance, is an obvious advantage. And by continuing with this research – even by investigating the most unlikely lines of enquiry – we are learning more about dolphins all the time.

---

sonar: the system that dolphins have for 'seeing' things through sound
telepathic: able to read people's minds

Ten arms and a giant's eye
Lee Krystek

The terrifying monster which grapples with Captain Nemo's submarine in Jules Vernes's *Twenty Thousand Leagues Under the Sea* is not complete fantasy. Giant squid do exist. But few have ever been seen and scientists know very little about their habits. This article describes what is known about this strange sea-monster.

Giant squid are **carnivorous molluscs** that have a long, torpedo-shaped body. At one end, surrounding a beak-like mouth strong enough to cut through steel cable, are five pairs of arms. One pair, thinner and longer than the rest, is used to catch food and bring it to the mouth. Just past the mouth are the eyes – eyes that are the largest in the animal kingdom, getting as big as eighteen inches across.

All squid move through the ocean using a jet of water forced out of the body by a **siphon**. They eat fish, other squid, and, in the case of the largest species, whales. The legend of the Kraken, a many-armed sea monster that could pull a whole ship under, may have been based on the giant squid.

The largest giant squid ever measured was discovered at Timble Tickle on November 2, 1878. Three fisherman were working not far off shore when they noticed a mass floating on the ocean they took to be wreckage. They investigated and found a giant squid had run aground. Using their anchor as a grappling hook they snagged the still living body and made it fast to a tree. When the tide went out the creature was left high and dry. After the animal died, the

---

carnivorous molluscs: meat-eating shellfish
siphon: a tube that pumps water

fishermen measured it and then chopped it up for dog meat. The body of the squid was twenty feet from tail to beak. The longer tentacles measured thirty-five feet and were tipped with four-inch suckers.

We know from eye-witness accounts that the giant squid feeds on whales. In October 1966, two lighthouse keepers at Danger Point, South Africa, observed a baby southern right whale under attack from a giant squid. For an hour and a half the monster clung to the whale trying to drown it as the whale's mother watched helplessly. 'The little whale could stay down for 10 to 12 minutes, then come up. It would just have enough time to spout – only two or three seconds – and then down again.' The squid finally won and the baby whale was never seen again.

Giant squid have been seen in battle with adult whales too. In 1965, a Soviet whaler watched a battle between a squid and a 40-ton sperm whale. In this case neither was victorious. The strangled whale was found floating in the sea with the squid's tentacles wrapped around the whale's throat. The squid's severed head was found in the whale's stomach.

Sperm whales eat squid and originally it had been thought that such battles were the result of a sperm whale taking on a squid that was just too large to be an easy meal. The incident with the *Brunswick* suggests otherwise. The *Brunswick* was a 15,000-ton auxiliary tanker owned by the Royal Norwegian Navy. In the 1930s it was attacked at least three times by giant squid. In each case the attack was deliberate as the squid would pull alongside the ship, pace it, then suddenly turn, run into the ship and wrap its tentacles around the hull. The encounters were fatal for the squid. Since the animal was unable to get a good grip on the ship's steel surface, it slid off and fell into the ship's propellers.

Apparently, for some unknown reason, the *Brunswick* looked like a whale to the squids. This suggests that the sperm whale is not always the aggressor in the battles. In fact, though many sperm whales have been captured, few of their stomachs seemed to contain parts of giant squids.

Unfortunately for scientists, but fortunately for the rest of us, humans do not meet up with giant squid very often. (There is at least one report from World War II of survivors of a sunken ship being attacked by a giant squid that ate one of the party.) Squid are thought to be open-water, deep, cold-sea creatures. Work by Dr Ole Brix, of the University of Bergen, indicates that the blood of squid does not carry oxygen very well at higher temperatures. A squid will actually suffocate in warm water.

Temperature also seems to affect the squid's buoyancy mechanism. Warm water will cause a giant squid to rise to the surface and not be able to get back down. With water temperature even higher at the surface, the squid may be doomed. It is not surprising then, that most squid groundings occur near where two ocean streams, one cold and one warm, meet.

How big can a squid get? Estimates based on damaged carcasses range up to one hundred feet. One story, though, suggests they might get even larger. One night during World War II a British Admiralty trawler was lying off the Maldive Islands in the Indian Ocean. One of the crew, AG Starkey, was up on deck, alone, fishing, when he saw something in the water. 'As I gazed, fascinated, a circle of green light glowed in my area of illumination. This green unwinking orb I suddenly realized was an eye. The surface of the water **undulated** with some strange disturbance. Gradually I realized that I was gazing at almost point-blank range at a huge squid.' Starkey walked the length of the ship finding the tail at one end and the tentacles at the other. The ship was over one hundred and seventy-five feet long.

---

undulated: became wavy

Activities

Baffling biology

1 All four pieces are news reports of strange events. Each has a clear headline to indicate what it is about. Which headline do you think is the most effective and why?

2 The dolphin report consists of two paragraphs. The first uses long sentences and passive verbs (verbs where the action is being done to the subject, for example, 'they were caught'). The second uses much shorter sentences and active verbs (verbs where the subject is doing the action, for example, 'they … guided it away from nearby rocks'). Why do you think the style changes like this?

3 In the ant report the author also uses active and passive verbs in referring to ants and people. What is the effect of doing this?

Big shot

1 This discursive text discusses various attempts at shooting a creature called a Bigfoot. It is structured into five paragraphs, the first introduces the issue and the rest describe failed attempts to shoot one. Unusually, there is no concluding recommendation. Why do you think the author decided not to include one?

2 Throughout the article the writer uses irony (saying one thing but meaning another) to make the reader question whether the Bigfoot actually exists. One example is in the title – it is ironic because hunters have bragged about shooting these creatures but actually have no proof, so they aren't big shots at all! Pick out another example like this and explain its effect.

3 Write a letter to the *Fortean Times*, arguing for or against hunters continuing to attempt to shoot a Bigfoot. Remember to set out your letter in an appropriate form and to adopt a formal tone. Introduce your argument and include evidence to support each of your points.

Meat-eating plants

1 In this explanation text, the naturalist David Attenborough is describing how a Venus' flytrap captures and devours its prey. He begins with a statement introducing the topic and goes on to list the steps the plant takes to obtain food. Identify these steps and list them in bullet points.

2 Notice how the steps are linked by temporal connectives (like 'then') and causal connectives (like 'because'). Try to find more words like this that link ideas in the text. Make a list of temporal connectives (for example, 'after') and a list of causal connectives (for example, 'in order').

3 Imagine what it must be like to be caught in a Venus' flytrap; write a description of the experience from an insect's point of view.

Things that go chomp in the night

1 In this report John Downer is trying to shock and horrify. He uses a number of techniques to do this. Find examples of each of these techniques in the text:

- emotive expression (words chosen for effect)
- metaphor (comparison by saying that something *is* something else)
- simile (comparison by saying that something *is like* something else)
- active verbs
- images.

2 Write a report like this about another household creature, using similar techniques.

Dolphin doctors

1 Mark Cawardine argues persuasively in favour of the healing power of dolphins. Which of his examples do you find the most convincing?

2 The author moves his argument from doubt to certainty by using words and phrases that are loaded or biased. For example 'suggests' implies a possibility only; 'difficult to demonstrate' means it can't be proved; both 'improved dramatically' and 'seem to benefit' suggest a noticeable improvement. Find other examples of these loaded expressions and explain their meaning.

3 Write a letter to your local MP arguing in favour of the government investing in more research into 'dolphin therapy'. You can use some of the techniques and arguments from the account.

Ten arms and a giant's eye

1 Use the information from the article to create a 'fact card' about the giant squid. Include information about sightings, and all the important statistics, such as the dimensions of the longest specimen ever recorded.

2 To add interest, the author includes stories of close encounters with giant squid. What is their effect on the reader?

Comparing the extracts

Which of the articles in this section did you enjoy most? In pairs, talk about your favourite and give reasons for your choices. You might have chosen a particular extract because:

- it was dramatic
- it was vividly described
- it was mysterious
- you found the subject-matter interesting
- you enjoyed the language

or for any other reason.

Section 3
Predator!

Since the days when we lived in caves, human beings have had a special respect for predators: creatures which kill and eat others in order to survive. Perhaps this is because we are predators ourselves and admire the skills of fellow hunters like the shark or rattlesnake. In this section you will meet some of the animal kingdom's most efficient killers. But first take a trip back in time . . .

Clash of the titans
Tim Haines

Walking with Dinosaurs was a thrilling television series for those of us who have often stared in awe at those huge fossil bones in the museum, trying to imagine what the real beasts must have looked like. One of the most dramatic moments in the series was the fight between a Torosaurus and the king of the dinosaurs, Tyrannosaurus Rex. When the sequence begins, two Torosaurus males are trying to catch the eye of a suitable mate.

Beside the lake, two evenly matched males have been **displaying** since sunrise. One is an experienced male, probably well over 50 years old. There is a long tear in the centre of his crest from a previous fight and the top of his back is heavily scarred from predator attacks. His rival is

---

displaying: showing off in front of each other

much younger, but almost as large. His crest sports two fine, dark eye-spots and his hide is considerably smoother and less scarred.

Gradually, their head-dipping and waggling comes to a halt; this is a bad sign. The older male bellows loudly. Then, suddenly, the young challenger lurches forward and they engage horns. The older bull stumbles back with the force of the attack. The two long forehead horns and the shorter nose horns lock together tightly. The two animals pause again, eye to eye, their heads lowered in combat. Torosaurus are large, heavy dinosaurs and their forelimb posture is slightly squat, making them slow but extremely stable. For each bull, it is like trying to shift a boulder the same size. With their heads firmly locked, they shift their weight to try to gain an advantage, and as they do, the strain on their necks is enormous.

As the mist thickens the bulls continue to try and subdue each other. Their horns rasp and grind as the headlock slips and tightens. Each grunts and snorts with the exertion of moving his opponent even the tiniest amount. After an hour, neither animal appears to have gained anything, but both are close to exhaustion. Suddenly the older bull **disengages** and retreats. The younger male pursues him for a few hundred metres, bucking his head and trumpeting his victory. Eventually he lets him go. Some distance from the herd the old Torosaurus stops and it becomes apparent why he has retreated. One of his forehead horns is hanging down and he is bleeding profusely over one eye.

Distracted by the pain of his broken horn, he fails to spot the approaching Tyrannosaurus until it is too late. The predator runs out of the mist and sinks his long, puncturing teeth into the old bull's flank. Anchoring himself with his right foot, he uses his short powerful neck to tear off a 30-kilogram slab of flesh. Tyrannosaurus is a large predator, but he is still lightly built compared to the Torosaurus. The last thing he wants to do is grapple with this massive prey. Having opened up a huge wound with that single bite, he backs off to wait for another opportunity.

Despite his injury, the Torosaurus swings round fast and faces his attacker. This is what makes these **herbivores** so difficult for lone predators to attack: in spite of their size, they can turn extremely quickly and present the predator with three long horns and a wide expanse of crest. Effectively, this is **stalemate** and Torosaurus have been known to continue grazing while keeping a hungry Tyrannosaurus at bay. However, for this

---

disengages: lets go of his hold

herbivores: plant-eaters

stalemate: deadlock; a situation where neither side can make a move

old bull the situation is very different. Confused and exhausted, he has a gaping wound in his side and one useless horn. He bellows in anger and pain and looks about for the rest of the herd. Unfortunately, they are now some distance away and can provide no protection for him. He tries to charge his tormentor, but stumbles to a halt in agony. The Tyrannosaurus stalks one way and then the other.

Eventually, the bull makes a fatal error. He panics and turns, trying to run back to the herd. The predator swiftly catches up with him and again sinks his teeth into his side. This time he shatters part of the hip bone. The Torosaurus stumbles and the Tyrannosaurus bites again. The Torosaurus gets up and faces his attacker. He no longer has the energy to turn and run, so he just stands rather unsteadily as shock and blood loss slowly overcome him. The Tyrannosaurus holds back, his mouth already dripping with the blood of several kilograms of Torosaurus meat. Realizing that his prey cannot go anywhere, he calls to the female in the Blanket Forest with a series of short, deep barks.

After half an hour, the old bull is still on his feet, and just before he loses consciousness, he finally gets to see the reason behind his death. A massive female Tyrannosaurus appears out of the mist. Scars disfigure one side of her face and she walks with the slightest limp. Her eyes are fixed on him and are deep red – a sign of age. The pitch of the male's call rises and he is careful not to place himself between his potential mate and the prey. She walks forward slowly, occasionally glancing at the male but making straight for the now **prostrate** Torosaurus. She sniffs the dying animal, long necklaces of saliva hanging from her mouth. She feeds, driving her long teeth into the flesh and ripping off large hunks

---

prostrate: lying face downwards

of skin, meat and even bone. This habit means that she frequently breaks her teeth. It is just as well they are not needed for chewing – she swallows the bulky mouthfuls she pulls off whole.

Silent hunters of the deep
Reader's Digest

Even before *Jaws*, sharks were the stuff of nightmares. Rodney Fox is a diver who has lived to tell the tale of a terrifying encounter with one of the deadliest predators known to humans – the 'great white'.

On 8 December 1963, Rodney Fox was competing in the South Australian Spearfishing Championships, having won the title the previous year.

Fox was in superb form, drifting, gliding, spearing his quick **elusive** targets with the practised ease of a born competitor. With an hour left, he looked likely to win the title again. He was one kilometre (1100 yds) offshore, drifting in for a shot at a **dusky morwong**, sure of the kill, his finger tensing on the trigger, when something huge hit his left side – 'it was like being hit by a train' – knocking the gun from his hand and tearing the mask from his face. His next impression was of speed, surging through the water faster then he had ever done, a gurgling roar in his ears, and of the easy, rhythmical power of the shark, holding him as a dog does a bone.

With his right arm he clawed for the shark's eyes; it released its grip and Fox instinctively thrust out his right arm to ward it off. The arm disappeared into the shark's mouth, **lacerating** the underside on the bottom row of teeth. As the horrified Fox jerked it out, the arm caught

---

elusive: good at getting away

dusky morwong: a type of fish found off the coast of Australia

lacerating: tearing

the upper jaw. **In extremity** men do amazing things: Fox, terrified of the open **maw**, tried to bear-hug the shark, to wrap his arms and legs around the **abrasive** skin, to **get a purchase** away from the teeth. It did not work – the shark was too big for him to hug.

He suddenly realised another need even more urgent than fending off the shark – air. He pushed away, kicked for the surface, gulped one breath and looked down on a scene that burnt itself into his memory. His mask gone, his vision blurred, he floated in a pink sea, and a few metres away was a pointed nose, and a mouth lined with razor sharp teeth, coming at him.

In desperation, Fox kicked with all his force at the shark. It was a **terminal gesture**, pointless, useless – but it worked: the shark turned from Fox, lunged for the buoy tied to his belt, swallowed it whole, then plunged for the deep. Fox, his ears roaring, reached for the quick-release clip on his belt. He could not find it. He realised the shark must have wrenched the belt around his body: the clip must be at his back. His lungs drained of air, his mind becoming fuzzy, he thought: that's it.

Then the impossible happened: the buoy rope snapped. Fox realised later that the shark must have bitten the rope when it attacked him. He floated to the surface, where his friend Bruce Farley and another man who had seen blood in the water pulled alongside in a boat. Fox's arms were so lacerated he could not raise them, so his friends gripped his wet suit and rolled him into the boat. Blood was pouring from his wet suit.

---

in extremity: in moments of great danger
maw: jaws, mouth and stomach
abrasive: rough and scratching
get a purchase: get a hold
terminal gesture: final act

Farley ran the boat onto the horseshoe reef. As they lifted Fox from the boat, loops of his intestines emerged from the hole in his belly; a bystander who had studied first aid for the police examinations pushed them back with his fingers. Fox was bundled into a car, straining to breathe – his left lung had collapsed. As the car sped for Adelaide, a friend, sick with anxiety, talked him on: 'You've got to keep breathing. Come on, keep trying, Rodney. Think of Kay and the baby. Keep going.' While his collapsed lung gurgled and Rodney heaved the air into his chest, his most vivid sensation was of swaying in the back of the car as it reached 150 km/h (95 mph). An ambulance dashed to meet them, and Fox was in hospital in Adelaide within an hour of leaving the water.

He recovered completely, and in 1964 Fox and Farley won the Australian Spearfishing Championship team's event.

The lethal touch
Mike and Tim Birkhead

A sting from a jelly-fish can be extremely painful, but it isn't usually life-threatening. The same cannot be said for the Portuguese man-o'-war, however. Named after an ancient fighting ship – and in its own way, just as dangerous – this sea creature has tentacles so venomous that one touch can result in sudden death. Mike and Tim Birkhead describe exactly what this strange-looking swimmer really is, and how it comes to be so deadly.

Many venomous creatures, in appearance innocent and harmless, inhabit the oceans. The Portuguese man-o'-war looks like a single organism but is in fact composed of numerous individual **polyps**, which resemble sea-anemones. Some of these are responsible for capturing and digesting food, while others form the gas-filled blue balloon which allows the animal to float on the sea's surface.

Each of the many feeding individuals in the colony possesses an extremely long tentacle which bears large numbers of stinging cells. Each stinging cell consists of a

polyps: tiny creatures with tube-shaped bodies

venom capsule and a reversible, barbed sting, evolved in order to capture prey such as surface-feeding fish.

When a mackerel or a flying fish, for example, **inadvertently** grazes a tentacle, hundreds of stinging cells fire and inject their venom into the victim, which is quickly paralysed and killed. The fish is then passed up into the mouths of the feeding individuals, and the **ingested** food is shared among all the other (non-feeding) members of the colony through a series of **cavities**.

If a human swimmer collides with a Portuguese man-o'-war, the consequences can be very dangerous. Severe pain, muscle **seizure** and heart failure may end in rapid death; or the pain may be so intense that the victim is unable to swim and drowns. However, if he or she survives the first half hour, there is a good chance of complete recovery.

---

venom: poison
inadvertently: without realising it
ingested: taken into the stomach
cavities: holes or openings
seizure: paralysis; the muscles are unable to work

The lurking watcher
Italo Calvino

Not all predators are terrifying monsters, like Tyrannosaurus; or potential man-eaters like the great white shark. Here the Italian novelist Italo Calvino describes the activities of a gecko, as it lies in wait for its prey in the home of Mr Palomar and his family.

On the terrace, the gecko has returned, as he does every summer. An exceptional observation point allows Mr Palomar to see him not from above, as we have always been accustomed to seeing geckos, treefrogs, and lizards, but from below. In the living room of the Palomar home there is a little show-case window and display case that opens onto the terrace; on the shelves of this case a collection of Art Nouveau vases is aligned; in the evening a 75-watt bulb illuminates the objects; a plumbago plant trails its pale blue flowers from the wall against the outside glass; every evening, as soon as the light is turned on, the gecko, who lives under the leaves on that wall, moves onto the glass, to the spot where the bulb shines, and remains motionless, like a lizard in the sun. Gnats fly around, also attracted by the light; the reptile, when a gnat comes within range, swallows it.

The most extraordinary thing are the claws, actual hands with soft fingers, all pad, which, pressed against the glass, adhere to it with their **minuscule** suckers: the five fingers stretch out like the petals of little flowers in a childish drawing, and when one claw moves, the fingers close like a flower, only to spread out again and flatten

---

minuscule: very small

against the glass, making tiny streaks, like fingerprints. At once delicate and strong, these hands seem to contain a potential intelligence, so that if they could only be freed from their task of remaining stuck there to the vertical surface they could acquire the talents of human hands, which are said to have become skilled after they no longer had to cling to boughs or press on the ground.

Bent, the legs seem not so much all knee as all elbow, elastic in order to raise the body. The tail adheres to the glass only along a central strip, from which the rings begin that circle it from one side to the other and make of it a sturdy and well-protected **implement**.

The throat is a limp sack's surface extending from the tip of the chin, hard and all scales like that of an alligator, to the white belly that, where it presses against the glass, also reveals a grainy, perhaps adhesive, speckling.

When a gnat passes close to the gecko's throat, the tongue flicks and engulfs, rapid and **supple** and **prehensile**, without shape, capable of assuming whatever shape. In any case, Mr Palomar is never sure if he has seen it or not seen it: what he surely does see, now, is the gnat inside the reptile's gullet: the belly pressed against the illuminated glass is transparent as if under X-rays; you can follow the shadow of the prey in its course through the **viscera** that absorb it.

Now a bewildered nocturnal butterfly comes within range. Will he overlook it? No, he catches this, too. His tongue is transformed into a butterfly net and he pulls it into his mouth. Will it all fit? Will he spit it out? Will he explode? No, the butterfly is there in his throat; it flutters, in a sorry state, but still itself, not touched by the insult of

---

implement: tool
supple: flexible, bending easily
prehensile: used for gripping
viscera: intestines and other organs inside the body

chewing teeth, now it passes the narrow limits of the neck, it is a shadow that begins its slow and troubled journey down along a swollen **oesophagus**.

The gecko, emerging from its **impassiveness**, gasps, shakes its **convulsed** throat, staggers on legs and tail, twists its belly, subjected to a severe test. Will this be enough for him, for tonight?

---

oesophagus: gullet; food-passage
impassiveness: calmness, stillness
convulsed: seized-up

Weapons control
David Attenborough

Most predators in the natural world inflict death and injury through their teeth, their claws or their venom. Humans, however, have developed all sorts of sophisticated weapons for wreaking destruction on their fellow beings. In this description, David Attenborough shows us that we can learn a great deal from rattlesnakes about 'restraint' – choosing not to use the devastating weapons in our possession.

Restraint in battle is particularly necessary among those animals that have **lethal** hunting weapons. Rattlesnakes are armed with one of the most **virulent** of all venoms. Injected by a stab from their long curved fangs, it will kill a small rodent in seconds.

These snakes too have their quarrels and in autumn, at the beginning of the breeding season, they fight among themselves. If they are not to kill one another, they must fight with great care.

When two rival males approach, face to face, they put the sides of their necks together and rear upwards. As their back halves continue to advance, their front sections rise higher and higher. They sway **sinuously** from side to side, partly propping one another up.

When their heads are two or even three feet above the ground, one of them makes a final lurch upwards and falls heavily on his opponent, slamming him to the ground.

---

lethal: deadly
virulent: poisonous
sinuously: curvily

They separate and then the wrestling starts again. The two may continue in this way for as long as half an hour, but at no stage does either attempt to bite his rival as he could very easily do.

So **innocuous** does this performance appear that it is often thought to be courtship between male and female and called a dance. And when the bout ends, it is not always clear to a human observer which is the winner. The consequence of the engagement, however, certainly seems to be that thereafter the two snakes keep out of one another's way. It is a **paradox**, but one that is not unknown in human affairs, that the most powerfully armed must necessarily in their quarrels be the most restrained.

---

innocuous: harmless

paradox: a statement which at first seems unlikely, but makes sense when you think about it

Activities

Clash of the titans

1 Although this event would have happened millions of years ago, this piece is written like an eyewitness account. This is because it is written in the present tense, for example 'the older male bellows loudly' and 'the young challenger lurches forward.' Why do you think the writer decided to use this form? What is the effect of doing so?

2 Pick out words which are used to communicate the size and strength of the Torosaurus and the stealth and viciousness of the Tyrannosaurus. Explain their meaning.

Torosaurus	Tyrannosaurus
Large – big Lurches	Predator – hunter Stalks

2 Write a commentary like Tim Haines', describing a combat between two animals. Remember to first set the scene, then describe the animals and use the present tense as if you are watching what is happening.

Silent hunters of the deep

1 This is an account of a shark attack on an Australian spear fisherman. It is written in the past tense, retelling events in chronological order. At the same time as the events are described, the writer tells you what the victim is thinking. Draw up a table listing the events and Fox's thoughts in two columns. Explain why the author uses this technique.

2 Imagine that Rodney Fox is interviewed soon after the attack for an Australian radio programme. Write the script for that interview, including questions and responses about the attack.

The lethal touch

1 This is an explanation text. Its purpose is to explain how
the Portuguese man-o'-war is a dangerous killing machine
made up of individuals specifically designed to co-operate
in capturing and killing prey. The text begins with a
general statement, then describes each part of the creature
in turn. It finishes with a description of the effect its sting
can have on a human being. Identify which paragraphs
make up each part of this structure and outline the key
points made.

2 Use the adjectives and adverbs in the passage to construct
a warning notice for bathers, warning them of the dangers
of a Portuguese man-o'-war and the possible effects of its
sting.

The lurking watcher

1 This is a piece of description that relies heavily on
comparisons for its effect. It uses both metaphor
(comparison by saying that something *is* something else)
and simile (comparison by saying that something *is like*
something else) to describe the appearance and behaviour
of the gecko. Pick out two metaphors and two similes from
the passage and explain what they describe and why they
are effective, for example:

metaphor = the claws, actual hands.
simile = five fingers stretch out like petals of little flowers.

2 Write your own piece about the appearance and
behaviour of an animal. Use the structure and language
techniques of Calvino's account of the gecko as a model.
Remember to set the scene: use the present tense and
describe the creature with adjectives, adverbs, descriptive
verbs, similes and metaphors. Anyone reading your piece
should be able to picture the animal.

Weapons control

1 This account of a conflict between two rattlesnakes uses two language techniques to create a profound effect. It uses an extended metaphor to compare the snakes' behaviour to human behaviour throughout the piece. It also uses paradox (a statement that seems to contradict itself). Explain what David Attenborough is trying to say about humans by using these techniques.

2 Think about other aspects of human behaviour that are similar to the behaviour of animals. Write a descriptive piece using an extended metaphor to show the similarity.

Comparing the extracts

1 Each of the extracts in this section is about a different kind of predator and takes a different view of predator behaviour: some are interested in predators which attack humans, for example; while others focus on conflicts between animals. Complete the following grid:

Extract	What it is about	What approach it takes
Clash of the titans		
Silent hunters of the deep		
The lethal touch		
The lurking watcher		
Weapons control		

a in the second column, write down the subject of the extract (the first one might be 'a tyrannosaurus preying on a Torosaurus').

b in the third column, write down the approach taken by the extract. The different approaches are listed here (not in the correct order!):

- an account of a human being attacked
- a commentary on a predator attacking a wounded prey
- a general description of a creature and its deadliness
- an account of the way predators avoid harming each other
- a description of a predator and an example of how it catches its prey.

2 Pick your favourite extract from this section and write a short review explaining what you like about it. In particular, try to explain how exactly the writer conveys the creature's predatory nature. For example, if you chose Italo Calvino's description of the gecko, you might refer to the way he compares different features of the animal to everyday things, and then write about his description of the way the gecko consumes its prey. Include short quotations from the extract to support the points you are making.

Section 4
The threatening universe

We cannot blame our distant ancestors for believing that volcanoes were angry gods and that eclipses foretold some terrible disaster; they are still awe-inspiring phenomena and a constant reminder of how powerless human beings really are. The extracts in this section provide evidence of the dangers which threaten us from space and from the Earth itself.

Impact Earth!
Rob Reather and DJ Dave

Most of the tiny meteorites which fall regularly to Earth are perfectly harmless. But, as this article suggests, a collision with one of the giant asteroids could be devastating.

The threat of asteroids

'In the year 2028, there is a great chance that the Earth will collide with an asteroid.' It was this information which sent ripples through the scientific community, waking up many scientists to the reality that a **cataclysmic** collision could occur. Even though it was later discovered that the asteroid XF11 actually posed little threat, it made many people aware that the Earth is just a sitting duck in the shooting gallery of space.

---

cataclysmic: totally destructive

What are asteroids?
About four and half billion years ago, our solar system
was one big huge cloud of gas and rocks, which was
slowly moving together under the influence of gravity.
As the material compressed together in the centre, the
surrounding gas and rocks started to form into other
separate lumps. It was from these that our solar system
was formed, with the central mass forming the sun and
the separate lumps forming the planets that would
encircle the sun. However, there was some material left
over, which formed the comets and asteroids that
threaten and amaze us today. Asteroids can be put into
two separate classes, the 'big' asteroids and the 'small'
meteorites. Meteorites are very common and cause
little worry among scientists. About 50,000 collide with
the Earth every year, most burning up in the
atmosphere. However, it is the big asteroids that cause
the most devastation and which worry most scientists.
There is a band of asteroids named the asteroid belt
which contains many huge asteroids, some being miles
in diameter. This belt is about 300 million miles
from the sun and acts as the boundary between the
inner solar system and the **outer solar system**.
Occasionally, an asteroid from another origin will cross
through this belt and 'knock' some of the larger
asteroids onto another orbit, possibly into a collision
course with Earth.

What will happen if an asteroid collides with us?
This is the ultimate doomsday worry, because if an
asteroid no more than one mile wide actually hit us, it
would mean the end of about 30% of the population. If an
asteroid like XFII did hit the planet, it would be the

---

inner . . . outer solar system: between the orbits of Mars and
Jupiter

equivalent of two million Hiroshima bombs, or 320,000 megatons of dynamite! This much energy would create a crater twenty miles in diameter, and would throw so much dust and material into the air that the sun would be blocked out for weeks. However, this isn't all that it would do. It would also **vaporise** any living creature within a hundred-mile radius of the collision site, and throw molten rocks hundreds of miles away from the point of impact.

Can asteroids be stopped?

This is the question that nobody is sure that we can answer just yet. At the moment **NASA** scientists are trying to create a method by which we can stop any space objects hitting us. The favoured idea is that we could detonate a nuclear explosive near the asteroid, deflecting it away from our planet. This would be a lot safer than actually trying to destroy the asteroid. If a nuclear device was planted on the asteroid, it would only shatter the asteroid and make the situation far worse. The second favoured idea is that a jet propulsion system could be placed on the asteroid and used to slowly turn the asteroid onto another orbit.

Research into past collisions shows that a large asteroid hits the Earth every 3000 years or so. The last big collision was about 3000 years ago . . .

---

the equivalent of two Hiroshima bombs: two million times as powerful as the atomic bomb which was dropped on the Japanese city of Hiroshima at the end of the Second World War

vaporise: turn into tiny particles

NASA: the North American Space Administration

The night the stars fell
Mark Littmann

One of the most impressive sights in the night sky is a shower of meteors or 'shooting stars', tiny particles from space, burning up as they race through the Earth's atmosphere. This account records how, in 1833, an American called Denison Olmsted witnessed an amazing spectacle in the night sky above his home in New Haven, Connecticut.

Denison Olmsted's left eye cracked open a slit. It was still night. He shut his eye. Something had awakened him. A noise from outside – sort of a muffled moan? Or was it the brightness of the moon visible through the curtains?

Suddenly both his eyes shot open and he sat bolt upright in bed. November 12 – no, now the 13th. It's new moon. The sky should be dark.

Then came a pounding on the door and the voice of his next-door neighbour, 'Denison. Denison. You must see this. Look out your window.'

He sprang from his bed – the few steps to his window and pulled the curtain aside. He looked. A shiver shot down his back.

In a moment he was heading out his door. He did not remember pulling his coat on over his nightclothes or wedging into his shoes. He stepped outside and looked up, his vision no longer framed and limited by his window – and a chill shuddered through him again. He saw not a meteor or two that would have made an ordinary night memorable. He saw dozens of shooting stars, fireballs, at every moment, in every direction. The sky was full of . . . fireworks. His first instinct was to duck, to fall to the

ground and cover his head to protect himself from these falling objects.

The appearance of these meteors was striking and splendid beyond anything he had ever witnessed.

There were so many, and yet – it was so . . . organised. It appeared that the meteors were all spreading out from a single point – high in the sky, near the **zenith**. Where in the star field? The falling stars made it hard to get his bearings. But it was Leo. The meteors were all radiating from the constellation Leo, the Lion. From the curve of the sickle-shaped pattern of stars that is supposed to be the Lion's mane.

But it wasn't that all the meteors started right at that point in Leo and raced away in all directions. Leo stood out because there were few meteors visible there. Only short streaks, sometimes bright. Or just momentary glowing dots, like fixed stars swelling in brightness and then fading away. No, Leo was the centre of this pageant because all the meteors he could see in every corner of the sky were streaking away from Leo. With so many of them, he could see it clearly. Even if a meteor trail started almost halfway across the sky from Leo, its trail was always away from Leo.

Olmsted wondered how widely this spectacle could be seen and what the reaction to it was. In that instant,

zenith: the point in the sky directly above you

he sensed that he, a college lecturer in astronomy, was privileged to be seeing an astronomical happening of historic magnitude. He had trained most of his life for such an opportunity. Would he be worthy? He redoubled his efforts to look closely and remember everything. He concentrated his thoughts on seeing the event scientifically.

Date. November 13, 1833.

Time. He didn't have his pocket watch. His neighbour did. It was 5:15 a.m.

Conditions. Excellent. No clouds. No Moon. Mild for November. No wind. Orion, Sirius, and Procyon in the southwest. Balancing that brightness were Venus and Saturn in the southeast. He could see them through the blizzard of falling stars primarily because they were among a tiny minority of stars that were not in motion.

He tried to focus on one meteor at a time, then another. It was difficult to do. Bright flashes caught by the corners of his eyes continuously distracted him. Each bright meteor left behind a vivid streak of light, ending in what sometimes seemed to be a puff of smoke, sometimes an explosion, sometimes . . . just vanishing.

And then he noticed – it was eerie – there was no noise from the heavens, no sound of explosion. He strained to listen more carefully. He did hear a noise, rising and falling with the bursts and lulls of the shower. It was . . . a moan. It was . . . people. A collective noise of shock and awe and – fear. People awakened as he had been from a sound sleep. Standing beneath a sight they had never seen – or been warned about – or imagined. Perhaps like no starfall ever seen. He wondered for just an instant whether this vision might yet be a dream.

Some meteors were brighter than others. Some brighter than Mars or Jupiter or even Venus, the planets that outshine the brightest of the true nighttime stars. His neighbour had seen one nearly as bright as the full moon, and seemingly that large in the sky.

When he first stepped outside and looked at the meteors, it appeared that they were all raining down from a point nearly straight up – the zenith –where Leo, the Lion, stood. Now, half an hour later, it occurred to Olmsted and his neighbours observing near him that the point of apparent radiation of the meteors had shifted. The meteors were still radiating from Leo, in fact, from near the star Gamma Leonis, but that **radiating point** had moved westward. The **radiant** of the meteor shower was moving westward **in synchronism with** the stars. The westward motion of the stars was created by the Earth spinning on its axis from west to east, once around in a day, causing the stars and Sun and Moon and planets to rise and set. Clearly, these shooting stars were not travelling with the Earth. They must have come from space, far beyond our planet.

Light was creeping up the eastern horizon. Dawn had come. The meteors were fewer and fewer now, but still they fell. Was the shower declining or was it just getting harder to see the shooting stars because of the twilight? He could still see bright ones. The fall of meteors must be continuing unseen into the morning light.

Not much time left. Notice everything. You never know what might be important.

The weather. On the evening of the 11th, it had rained **copiously**, giving way on the 12th to gusty winds from the west. The skies cleared by evening and he had seen . . . a few falling stars . . . before bedtime. And now, the weather was perfect. Any connection? Time for that later.

---

radiating point; or **radiant**: the point from which the meteors seemed to be coming

in synchronism with: in time with

copiously: very heavily

Had anything like this **deluge** of meteors ever happened before? It seemed to him he had read about something like this. He thanked the neighbour who had awakened him and said good night – good morning, rather – to the other citizens and rushed inside to begin writing while the memory was still fresh. He might just have time to dash off a brief report and offer it to the newspaper, ending with a request for accounts from other observers.

Now where had he read about a previous extraordinary meteor storm? A travel book by Humboldt. He owned a copy. Yes, there it was, near the beginning of his travels in South America. Humboldt and Bonpland saw a meteoric spectacle from Cumaná in 1799. Huh. Look at that. The meteors fell in the early morning hours of the 12th of November. That was worth noting.

Olmsted delivered his impressions to the *New Haven Daily Herald* and his article was published that same day, including his hope to hear from other observers.

The response overwhelmed him. Other newspapers across the young nation had picked up his report and Denison Olmsted, 42 years old, professor of mathematics and natural philosophy at Yale College, found himself the clearinghouse for information and interpretation of the stars that fell on November 13, 1833. It was to be the defining moment of his career.

Afterword
This storm of shooting stars is now called the Leonids, because it appears to come from the constellation Leo.

---

deluge: heavy fall

The death of the Sun
Arthur C Clarke

Our Sun, the star which provides us with warmth and life, is – like the rest of us – growing older, using up its hydrogen fuel at a rate of half a billion tons per second. This article describes what will happen when, after perhaps five billion years, our yellow star begins to shrink and becomes a 'red dwarf'.

When the Sun shrinks to a dull red dwarf, it will not be dying. It will just be starting to live – and *everything that has gone before will be merely a fleeting **prelude** to its real history*.

For a red dwarf, because it is so small and so cool, loses energy at such an incredibly slow rate that it can stay in business for *thousands* of times longer than a normal-sized white or yellow star. We must no longer talk in billions but of **trillions** of years if we are to measure its life-span. Such figures are, of course, inconceivable. (For that matter, who can think of a million years?) But we can nevertheless put them into their right perspective if we relate the life of a star to the life of a man.

On this scale, the Sun is but a week old. Its flaming youth will continue for another month; then it will settle down to a **sedate** adult existence which may last at least eighty years.

Life has existed on this planet for two or three days of the week that has passed; the whole of human history lies within the last second, and there are eighty years to come.

---

prelude: lead-in, introduction

trillions: a million million million (1, followed by 18 noughts!)

sedate: quiet and peaceful

Mountains of fire

You have probably seen television programmes which show volcanoes erupting. No film, however, can give a real impression of their awesome destructive power. In these extracts, David Attenborough describes the most devastating volcanic eruption in recorded history; and Bill McQuire and Christopher Kilburn tell what it was like to visit the countryside around a volcano only a few days after it had erupted.

The power of Krakatau
David Attenborough

It was one of the Indonesian volcanoes that produced the most **catastrophic** explosion yet recorded. In 1883, a small island named Krakatau, 7 kilometres long by 5 kilometres wide, lying in the straits between Sumatra and Java, began to emit clouds of smoke. The eruptions continued with increasing severity day after day.

Ships sailing nearby had to make their way through immense rafts of **pumice** that floated on the surface of the sea. Ash rained down on their decks and electric flames played along their rigging. Day after day, enormous quantities of ash, pumice and lava blocks were thrown out from the crater, accompanied by deafening explosions. But the **subterranean** chamber from which all this material was coming was slowly emptying.

At 10 a.m. on 28 August, the rock roof of the chamber, insufficiently supported by lava beneath, could bear the

catastrophic: extremely destructive
pumice: solidified lava
subterranean: underground

weight of the ocean and its floor no longer. It collapsed. Millions of tons of water fell on to the molten lava in the chamber and two-thirds of the island tumbled on top of it.

The result was an explosion of such magnitude that it produced the loudest noise ever to echo round the world in recorded history. It was heard quite distinctly over 3000 kilometres away in Australia. Five thousand kilometres away, on the small island of Rodriguez, the commander of the British **garrison** thought it was the sound of distant gunfire and put out to sea. A tempest of wind swept away from the site and circled the earth seven times before it finally died away.

Most catastrophic of all, the explosion produced an immense wave in the sea. As it travelled towards the coast of Java, it became a wall of water as high as a four-storey house. It picked up a naval gunboat, carried it bodily nearly 2 kilometres inland and dumped it on top of a hill. It overwhelmed village after village along the thickly populated coast. Over 36,000 people died.

A colourless world
Bill McQuire and Christopher Kilburn

In the eyes of the witnesses there is no panic, just total shock, as if the **fundamental** laws of life have been called into doubt. Around us, nothing human remains: a country of **phantoms**, a countryside with no colour. Uniformly grey. The shapes are still there but they have been softened, and all covered in grey. There is no daylight, just darkness – as if the sky were closing down on us.

---

garrison: troops stationed to defend a town or fortress
fundamental: basic
phantoms: ghosts

It is 14.00hrs on 22 June 1991 and we are in the eighth day of the eruption of Mt Pinatubo.

It's raining. It's raining grey; it's raining **pulverised** rock. Above our heads, an enormous cloud 17,000m (55,750ft) tall fills the sky and blocks all the light. The fine ashes fall, covering everything; slowly, **insidiously**. We are watching a slow suffocation, a complete **obliteration** of life. It's a progressive disappearance, as if **organic** life were slowly changing to mineral. And in the same way as the light has faded, so has all sound disappeared. There's not a whisper, not a sound: men and animals move like ghosts.

Further on, at the heart of **the evacuated zone**, we reach an old village. It's like a theatre set: houses, beds, tables and chairs, pots and pans . . . everything is there – waiting for the actors. This impression of unreality is underlined by the absence of colour. The village is covered under a thick **shroud** of white ashes. But there is still something more terrible: under the shroud, it has been **carbonised**!

Devastating **pyroclastic flows** ran down the side of Pinatubo and one of them stopped a few hundred metres from here. The village felt the heat of the boiling clouds which burned everything. There's not a hint of green: the heads of the palm trees are deformed by the weight of ashes and are **desiccated**, roasted by the breath of the volcano. And in the houses, the plastic cups and plates have melted on the shelves.

---

pulverised: turned to powder or dust

insidiously: craftily, without anyone noticing

obliteration: wiping out

organic: animal or plant

the evacuated zone: the area from which people have been moved

shroud: deathly veil

carbonised: turned to carbon or charcoal

pyroclastic flows: streams of burning lava and other molten material

desiccated: completely dried out

Activities

Impact Earth!

1 The form and style of this magazine article are partly informative and partly sensational. Pick out examples of the following features and identify which is intended to inform and which to sensationalise:

a) attention-grabbing headline; b) simple sub-headings; c) quotations; d) simplification; e) qualifying statements (statements that provide more information about a point); f) modifying statements (statements that change or lessen the strength of a point); g) facts and figures; h) adjectives; i) examples;   j) rhetorical questions.

2 Now rewrite this as a tabloid news report telling how scientists have just spotted a huge asteroid heading straight for Earth. You will need to overplay the sensational techniques and drop the informative features.

The night the stars fell

1 In this recount text the author tries to set the scene in the first few paragraphs. He also aims to create a sense of mystery and tension using language techniques, for example: 'Something had awakened him'. Find other examples like these in the orientation section of the passage. What effect do they have on the reader?

2 Look at the part where the sightings are described, and write the notes that Olmsted might have taken as the basis of his news report. Include:

- first impressions of the meteors' appearance
- where they came from
- date, time and weather conditions
- how long the shower lasted.

Use your notes to write the report that Olmsted might have sent to the *Newhaven Daily Herald*. Remember to include answers to the questions What, Who, When, Where and How?

The death of the Sun

1 This article is written using a mixture of tenses: past, present and future.

  a Pick out examples of verbs written in each tense.

Past	Present	Future

  b Explain why the author uses three tenses in this text.

2 In the last two paragraphs the author uses an analogy (a comparison technique). He compares the lifespan of the Sun with the life of a human being. Why do you think he does this? Try to think of an analogy to help explain another difficult idea.

Mountains of fire

1 Both these accounts paint a realistic picture of the effects of a volcanic eruption by using expressions that appeal to our senses. Find as many examples as you can in the texts that appeal to the reader's senses. For example the first extract refers to the explosions as 'deafening', making it clear to the reader how loud they actually are.

2 Try to write a similar description of something you have experienced or witnessed, using expressions that appeal to the senses. It might be extreme weather conditions, or a dramatic or frightening event. Choose carefully words that describe how it looked, how it felt, what you heard, the taste of it or the smell of it, and use them in your account.

Comparing the extracts

1 What similarities can you find between these extracts?
Draw a grid like the one below and put a tick under the
title of the extracts which you think include the ideas listed
in the left-hand column.

Ideas	Impact Earth!	The night the stars fell	The death of the Sun	Mountains of fire
The universe is immense				
The Earth will not last for ever				
Humans are powerless against natural forces				
A major disaster could hit us soon				
Witnessing these phenomena makes us full of wonder				

2 Write the opening two or three paragraphs of a short
story based on one of the following situations:

- an asteroid heading for Earth
- an unusually brilliant meteor-storm
- a dying planet
- an erupting volcano.

Use facts and ideas from the extracts to make your writing
vivid and realistic.

One great step . . .

Scientists and technologists don't make discoveries on their own: they all use the knowledge gained by the men and women who came before them. But every now and then an advance is made which does become associated with one particular person or team of people. And that is certainly what happened with the invention of the telephone, the first powered flight, and the Apollo mission to land humans on the moon.

Distant voices

Christine Moorcroft and Magnus Magnusson

Alexander Graham Bell, known in his family as Aleck, had always been interested in the human voice and devoted his time as a young man to teaching deaf children to speak. But he had another ambition: to find a way of using electricity to send messages along wires. This account is taken from a book written for young readers. The scene is America in the 1870s.

One of Aleck's deaf pupils was 16-year-old Mabel Hubbard. Her father was very rich.

One day, Aleck noticed that, when he sang a note into the piano while pressing its pedal, the wires inside it vibrated and made the same sound. He thought he could make the wires repeat all the sounds of a word and a sentence. He was very excited!

Aleck showed Mr Hubbard, Mabel's father, the piano trick. He told Mr Hubbard about his ideas for the talking telegraph. Mr Hubbard was very interested. He talked to Mr Sanders and they agreed to pay Aleck to invent the talking telegraph.

Aleck worked hard on his idea for the 'telephone'. Before long he knew he would be able to make a machine which would let people talk to one another across long distances.

In 1874, he met a man called Thomas Watson, who worked in the electrical shop where he bought the things he needed for his inventions. Thomas understood electricity, so Aleck asked him to be his assistant.

They set up the machines in the electrical shop. The story goes that, in July 1875, Aleck was working on the machine upstairs when he knocked some liquid onto the table. He shouted into his machine "Mr Watson, come here quickly!' Thomas, who was downstairs, heard a sound come through the machine! It worked!

The next step was to make voices sound clearer. On 10 March 1876, Aleck spoke into the machine and at the other end of the wire Thomas could hear what he said.

Aleck wrote to his father to tell him the good news. He knew that one day soon people would be able to talk to one another without leaving their homes. All this time, other people had been trying to invent a telephone. But Alexander Graham Bell was the first to do it.

Into the air
Orville Wright

The Wright brothers, Wilbur and Orville, had been fascinated by the idea of powered flight since childhood, when their father had given them a toy helicopter. Using the skills they had acquired in their bicycle-repair business, they had, by December 1902, designed and built the first flying-machine, a biplane with a forty-foot wingspan. After an unsuccessful attempt with Wilbur at the controls, it was now Orville's turn. This is from an account he wrote in 1913.

With all the knowledge and skill acquired in thousands of flights in the last ten years, I would hardly think today of making my first flight on a strange machine in a 27-mile wind, even if I knew that the machine had already been flown and was safe. After these years of experience, I look with amazement upon our **audacity** in attempting flights with a new and untried machine under such circumstances. Yet faith in our calculations and the design of the first machine, based upon our tables of air pressure, obtained by months of careful laboratory work, and confidence in our system of control developed by three years of actual experiences in balancing gliders in the air had convinced us that the machine was capable of lifting and maintaining itself in the air, and that, with a little practice, it could be safely flown.

Wilbur having used his turn in the unsuccessful attempt on the fourteenth, the right to the first trial now belonged to me. After running the motor a few minutes

audacity: boldness

to heat it up, I released the wire that held the machine to the track, and the machine started forward into the wind. Wilbur ran at the side of the machine, holding the wing to balance it on the track.

Unlike the start on the fourteenth, made in a calm, the machine, facing a 27-mile wind, started very slowly. Wilbur was able to stay with it till it lifted from the track, after a forty-foot run. One of the **life-saving** men snapped the camera for us, taking a picture just as the machine had reached the end of the track and had risen to a height of about two feet. The slow forward speed of the machine over the ground is clearly shown in the picture by Wilbur's attitude. He stayed along beside the machine without any effort.

The course of the flight up and down was exceedingly **erratic**, partly due to the irregularity of the air and partly to lack of experience in handling this machine.

---

life-saving men: rescue crew
erratic: jerky and unsteady

The control of the front rudder was difficult on account of its being balanced too near the centre. This gave it a tendency to turn itself when started, so that it turned too far on one side and then too far on the other. As a result, the machine would rise suddenly to about ten feet, and then as suddenly dart for the ground.

This flight lasted only 12 seconds, but it was nevertheless the first in the history of the world in which a machine carrying a man had raised itself by its own power into the air in full flight, had sailed forward without reduction of speed, and had finally landed at a point as high as that from which it started.

The Eagle has landed

Nobody who was watching television at 3.18pm (Houston time) on 20 July 1969 will ever forget Neil Armstrong reporting over a crackly radio, 'The Eagle has landed'. The lunar module from the Apollo 11 spacecraft had touched down on the moon, and it would be only a matter of seconds before a human being would actually set foot on the moon's surface. In these extracts Neil Armstrong and his fellow-astronaut Buzz Aldrin describe their amazing experiences.

Approaching their destination
Neil Armstrong

The most dramatic **recollections** I had were the sights themselves. Of all the spectacular views we had, the most impressive to me was on the way to the moon, when we flew through the shadow. We were still thousands of miles away, but close enough so that the moon almost filled our circular window. It was eclipsing the sun, from our position, and the **corona** of the sun was visible around the limb of the moon as a gigantic lens-shaped or saucer-shaped light, stretching out to several lunar diameters. It was magnificent, but the moon was even more so. We were in its shadow, so there was no part of it illuminated by the sun. It was illuminated only by earthshine. It made the moon appear blue-grey, and the entire scene looked decidedly three-dimensional.

recollections: memories
corona: circle of light or gases

I was really aware, visually aware, that the moon was in fact a sphere, not a disc. It seemed almost as if it were showing us its roundness, its similarity in shape to our earth, in a sort of welcome. I was sure that it would be a hospitable host. It had been awaiting its first visitors for a long time.

Moonscape
Neil Armstrong

The sky is black, you know. It's a very dark sky. But it still seemed more like daylight than darkness as we looked out the window. It's a peculiar thing, but the surface looked very warm and inviting. It looked as if it would be a nice place to take a sunbath. It was the sort of situation in which you felt like going out there in nothing but a swimming suit to get a little sun. From the cockpit, the surface seemed to be tan. It's hard to account for that, because later, when I held this material in my hand, it wasn't tan at all. It was black, grey and so on. It's some kind of lighting effect, but out the window the surface looks much more like light desert sand than black sand.

Gravity and gunpowder
Buzz Aldrin

The moon was a very natural and very pleasant environment in which to work. It had many of the advantages of **zero-gravity**, but it was in a sense less *lonesome* than zero G,

---

zero gravity: state of complete weightlessness

where you always have to pay attention to securing attachment points to give you some means of leverage. In one-sixth gravity, on the moon, you had a distinct feeling of being *somewhere*, and you had a constant, though at many times **ill-defined**, sense of direction and force . . .

As we **deployed** our experiments on the surface we had to **jettison** things like **lanyards**, retaining fasteners, etc., and some of these we tossed away. The objects would go away with a slow, lazy motion. If anyone tried to throw a baseball back and forth in that atmosphere he would have difficulty, at first, **acclimatising** himself to that slow, lazy **trajectory**; but I believe he could adapt to it quite readily.

Odour is very **subjective**, but to me there was a distinct smell to the lunar material – pungent, like gunpowder or spent cap-pistol caps. We carted a fair amount of lunar dust back inside the vehicle with us, either on our suits and boots or on the conveyor system we used to get boxes and equipment back inside. We did notice the odour right away.

---

ill-defined: difficult to pin down or put into words
deployed: arranged, spread out
jettison: throw away
lanyards: short ropes for attaching to things
acclimatising: getting used to
trajectory: the path an object takes when it is thrown
subjective: personal

Activities

Distant voices

1 This is an historical account of the invention of the telephone written for young readers. It is written in the past tense and describes events in chronological order. It also uses the kind of language that you would expect to see in a story so that younger readers will be able to follow what is happening. Pick out examples of this storytelling technique, for example, 'One day…'

2 Scientists have always had to find new words for their inventions. *Telephone* comes from two ancient Greek words: *tele*, which means 'far', and *phone*, which means 'sound'. So a telephone is a 'far-sound'.

Here are some other word-parts taken from ancient Greek and Latin. Use them to work out answers to the questions which follow:

graph = to record, to write
scope = to see
auto = self
bio = life

a Which inventions enabled people to:
  - see a long distance (a 'far-see')?
  - hear recordings (a 'sound-record')?
  - send messages along wires (a 'far-record')?

b What is the name given to a book that
  - is about someone's life (a 'life-write')
  - someone writes about their own life (a 'self-life-write')?

c What is an *autograph*? Where does the word come from?
  - Where does the word *television* come from?
  - When Alexander Graham Bell wrote to the United States Patent Office about his invention, he actually called it an *autograph telegraph*. Another inventor called it a *teleautograph*. What did these words mean?

3 Do some research on another inventor, by looking in an encyclopedia. Then write a short account of how they came to make their breakthrough. If you decide to write it for younger readers, like this account, remember to keep the language and ideas simple.

Into the air

1 This is an account of the very first powered flight engineered by the Wright brothers. It is written by the pilot Orville Wright. He writes in the first person and the past tense. In the first paragraph of his account he looks back on the flight. He then goes on to describe what happened in the next three paragraphs and puts it in context as the first manned flight in the final paragraph. Why do you think he writes it in this way?

2 Imagine that this first flight were being recorded live on radio. Write a script of the commentary, based on Orville's own description, then draft an interview with Orville and his brother Wilbur. You might ask them to give more details about speed and distance, for example. When you have completed your radio script, you could perform it in small groups.

The Eagle has landed

1 In Neil Armstrong's account of his journey towards the moon he uses a literary device called 'personification' (giving an inanimate object human qualities). What is the effect of using this device?

2 In his second account Armstrong likens the lighting effect on the moon to sunbathing and Aldrin uses baseball and gunpowder to illustrate what it felt like to be in one-sixth gravity and to describe the smell on the moon. Why do you think the astronauts use these kinds of comparisons?

3 Neil Armstrong's first words on the moon were: 'One small step for a man. One great step for mankind.' (If you listen

to the recording, it sounds as though he says 'One small step for *man* ...', which doesn't make as much sense.) In pairs, discuss what point you think Armstrong was trying to make. Then decide what you might have said in his position: what message would you have wanted the world to hear?

Comparing the extracts

1 In small groups, discuss which of the achievements in this section you think has proved to be the most important to human beings – the invention of the telephone, the development of powered flight, or space research. What has each of the achievements enabled us to do which was impossible before?

2 Draw up *Question and Answer* columns to appear in a popular magazine on one of the following: Alexander Graham Bell, Orville Wright, Wilbur Wright, or Neil Armstrong. The questions which are often asked are: 'What was your greatest moment?' 'What would you have done differently?' 'What would your motto be?' It will help to do some more background research on your chosen figure before you start to work out which other questions you are going to ask.

Section 6

The big idea: Charles Darwin

There have been very few men and women whose discoveries have forced people to change their view of the world and their beliefs about where they came from. But one person who did succeed in doing just that was the nineteenth-century scientist Charles Darwin. In this section you can read about Darwin and his discoveries in extracts from:

1 an encyclopedia
2 an account of a key episode in Darwin's life
3 Darwin's own famous book *The Origin of Species* and
4 a biography.

Darwin's life
The Oxford Children's Encyclopedia

This article is from an encyclopedia for young readers. It gives an overview of Darwin's life and work.

Darwin, Charles
Born 1809 in Shrewsbury, England
Best known for his theory of evolution by natural selection, Darwin was a great biologist who studied many other things including coral reefs, barnacles, earthworms and orchids.
Died 1882 aged 73

Charles Robert Darwin was born into a famous family. His grandfather, Erasmus Darwin, was a doctor who also wrote poetry and philosophy. His mother was the daughter of Josiah Wedgwood, the pottery manufacturer.

As a boy, Charles Darwin did not care much for school. Instead, he enjoyed gardening and looking at plants and animals. His father, a doctor, decided that Charles should study medicine. But Charles found that he could not stand the sight of blood, and hated the brutality of the treatments given in those days before anaesthetics. After two years he went to Cambridge to study classics instead but was more interested in geology and botany.

He became the friend of the professor of botany, who suggested, after Darwin had only just scraped through his final exams, that he would be a suitable person to go as the naturalist and companion to the captain of a naval survey ship, HMS *Beagle*. Charles set sail on 27 December 1831 for what was to be a five-year journey.

He suffered terribly from seasickness throughout the voyage, but when the weather was good he made notes on everything seen from the ship and collected small sea creatures in a towing net. When the *Beagle* spent time in ports, Darwin was able to get ashore. He saw something of the Amazon rainforests and the deserts of Patagonia. In Chile he journeyed up into the Andes and observed the changes in the countryside made by a recent large earthquake.

But the most important part of the voyage turned out to be the few weeks that the *Beagle* spent in the Galápagos Islands, which lie on the Equator, about 1,000 km (600 miles) from the coast of South America. They have plants and animals that are found nowhere else. Darwin was struck one day when a resident of the Galápagos said that he could say, without being told, which island a particular tortoise came from, as each island had its own sort. Why, wondered Darwin, should this be?

When he got home, Darwin realized that some of the birds from the Galápagos were like the tortoises in being closely related to each other but different in the shapes of their beaks. Yet the birds from any one one island were similar. They were all rather like some small birds that live on the South American mainland, and Darwin decided that some of these must have reached the Galápagos accidentally, perhaps by being blown off course during a storm, and had evolved (changed) in their new home.

Darwin began to investigate all the animals he could. After many years he eventually came to a conclusion based on four observations.

1 All individual animals and plants are different from all of the rest.
2 In spite of the differences between individuals, children tend to look like their parents.
3 All living things produce very large numbers of young.
4 In spite of this, the numbers of all living things stay much the same from one year to the next.

These four observations led him to one conclusion: most of the young animals must die, and the ones that survived were those best fitted to their way of life. If, every now and again, an animal was born which had some feature that gave it an advantage, it would survive, and so would its offspring that were like it. Selection would work, rather like a farmer selecting the animals that he wished to breed from, but in this case it would be natural selection that would cause a population to evolve.

Darwin hesitated to publish his ideas, possibly because he knew they would upset many people. But in 1859 his book called *The Origin of Species* came out. It caused an uproar, as it contradicted the ideas found in the Bible. But few people nowadays doubt the basic truth of Darwin's arguments.

A year or so after his return from the *Beagle* voyage Darwin's health declined until eventually he was an almost permanent invalid. In spite of this, he seems to have retained his good temper and kind disposition. He had married his cousin Emma in 1839, and they lived in Downe in Kent, where they had ten children.

Voyage of discovery
Alan Moorehead

The turning-point in Darwin's life was his five-year voyage (1831–1836) as the naturalist on board a government survey ship, HMS *Beagle*, under Captain Fitzroy. It was this voyage, which took him to South America and the islands of the Pacific, which furnished him with a wealth of startling new evidence about the natural world and its history. In 1832 the *Beagle* called in to Bahia Blanca, a remote port in Argentina, and Darwin set off along the desolate beach to see what he could find. The watching soldiers from the local garrison were understandably uneasy . . .

The soldiers were suspicious of the *Beagle* at first – she might be smuggling arms to the tribes or perhaps spying for a foreign power – and in particular they did not like the looks of *El Naturalista,* **Don Carlos** Darwin. What was a naturalist? What was he doing coming ashore with his two pistols stuck in his belt and his geological hammer in his hand? They followed him along the beach and watched with distrust when he began to hack away at some old bones embedded in a cliff.

Punta Alta, the scene of some of Darwin's greatest discoveries, both on this first visit and a year later, was a low bank on the shore some twenty feet in height, composed of shingle and gravel with a **stratum** of muddy reddish clay running through it. The fossilised bones were found in the gravel at the foot of this cliff and were

---

El Naturalista, **Don Carlos**: The Naturalist, Mr Charles
stratum/strata: layer/layers

scattered over an area of about 200 yards square. At first Darwin could not make out what it was he was unearthing; there was a tusk, a pair of huge claws, a hippopotamus-like skull, a great scaly **carapace** turned to stone. One thing these relics shared in common, apart from their strangeness: they were all immense, all much bigger than the bones of any similar animal alive today.

Up to this time – 1832 – very little research had been made into the **palaeontology** of South America. Half a century before, the skeleton of a *Megatherium*, a giant sloth, had been found, in the Argentine and sent to Madrid, and von Humboldt and a few other travellers had unearthed some mastodon teeth, but little else was known, so it is easy to understand Darwin's excitement as these huge prehistoric forms began to take shape. 'The great size of the bones of the Megatheroid animals,' he wrote in his journal, 'is truly wonderful'.

He and Covington set to work with pick-axes at Punta Alta. Time was short and Darwin became engrossed in his searches. '**Staid** the night at Punta Alta in order for 24 hours of bone searching. Very successful with the bones, passed the night pleasantly.' More and more fossilised skeletons came to light, and were stacked upon the beach, and Darwin began to realise that he was dealing here with creatures that were virtually unknown to modern zoology, and which had vanished from the earth many millennia ago. There were parts of that giant sloth, the monster that had once reached up its claws to feed on the tree-tops, and two other beasts, equally large and closely related, the *Megalonyx* and the *Scelidotherium* (he got a nearly perfect skeleton of this last one). Then there were the *Toxodon*, an animal like a

---

carapace: upper shell
palaeontology: the study of extinct creatures
'**Staid** . . .': Darwin's spelling of '**stayed**'

hippopotamus and 'one of the strangest animals ever discovered'; the giant armadillo; the tusk of a *Mylodon*, an extinct elephant; a *Macrauchenia*, 'remarkable **quadruped**', and a guanaco (or wild llama) as big as a camel.

For Darwin the important thing about these creatures was that, being different species, they nevertheless closely resembled their much smaller counterparts alive in the world today; the tiny sloths that lived in the trees, the little burrowing armadillo, the delicate guanaco. 'This wonderful relationship in the same continent between the dead and the living will, I do not doubt, hereafter throw more light on the appearance of **organic beings** on earth and their disappearance from it.' Where had these great beasts been at the time of **the Flood**?

Perhaps most mysterious of all was the discovery of the bones of a horse. When the Spanish **conquistadores** arrived in the sixteenth century the horse was unknown in South America. Yet here was definite proof that the animals had existed in the remote past. Did all this mean that the various species were constantly changing and developing, and that those which failed to adjust themselves to their environment died out? If this were so, then the present inhabitants of the world were very different from those that God had originally created; indeed, there could even be some doubt whether the Creation could have taken place within a single week; creation was a continuous process and it had been going on for a long time.

One problem that puzzled Darwin was that of the relation between the vegetation of the country and the number of animals; he finally made up his mind that

---

quadruped: four-legged creature
organic beings: living creatures
the Flood: the great flood described in the Bible
conquistadores: the invading Spanish soldiers

quantity of vegetation was not essential, and as for the quality 'the ancient rhinoceros might have roamed over the **steppes** of central Siberia even in their present condition'. There was no evidence at all, he said, to support the idea that luxuriant tropical vegetation was necessary to these animals.

What then had **exterminated** so many species? 'Certainly no fact in the long history of the world is so startling as the wide and repeated extermination of its inhabitants.' He ruled out the possibility that changes in climate might have caused this extermination, and after considering many theories came to the conclusion that the isthmus of Panama might once have been submerged. He was right. For seventy million years there was no **isthmus of Panama**, South America was an island, and these great animals evolved in isolation. When the isthmus arose and North America was joined to South America the fate of these curious and largely helpless beasts was sealed.

When Darwin took his specimens back on board the *Beagle* Wickham was disgusted at the '**bedevilment**' of his clean decks and **railed** against 'the damned stuff'. FitzRoy later on recalled 'our smiles at the apparent rubbish he frequently brought on board'. But to Darwin this was no light matter, and it must have been about this time that he first began to argue with FitzRoy about the **authenticity** of the story of the Flood. How had such enormous creatures got aboard the Ark?

---

steppes: great plains
exterminated: killed off
isthmus of Panama: the thin strip of land joining North America to South America
bedevilment: spoiling
railed: complained
authenticity: truth or genuineness

The giant tortoise
Charles Darwin

When Darwin returned to England after his momentous voyage, he set about writing up his findings. Here is his description of the giant tortoise which had become extinct everywhere except the Galápagos Archipelago (group of islands).

I will first describe the habits of the tortoise (*Testudo indicus*) which has been so frequently **alluded to**. These animals are found, I believe, in all the islands of the Archipelago. Some individuals grow to an immense size: Mr Lawson, an Englishman, who had at the time of our visit charge of the colony, told us that he had seen several so large, that it required six or eight men to lift them from the ground; and that some had **afforded** as much as 200 pounds of meat. The old males are the largest, the females rarely growing to so great a size. The male can readily be distinguished from the female by the greater length of its tail.

The tortoise is very fond of water, drinking large quantities, and wallowing in the mud. The larger islands alone possess springs, and these are always situated towards the central parts, and at a considerable elevation. The tortoises, therefore, which frequent the lower districts, when thirsty, are obliged to travel from a long distance. Hence broad and well-beaten paths radiate off in every direction from the wells even down to the sea-coast; and the Spaniards by following them up, first discovered the watering-places.

alluded to: referred to
afforded: provided

When I landed at Chatham Island, I could not imagine what animal travelled so **methodically** along the well-chosen tracks. Near the springs it was a curious spectacle to behold many of these great monsters; one set eagerly travelling onwards with outstretched necks, and another set returning, after having drunk their fill. When the tortoise arrives at the spring, quite regardless of any spectator, it buries its head in the water above its eyes, and greedily swallows great mouthfuls, at the rate of about ten in a minute. The inhabitants say each animal stays three or four days in the neighbourhood of the water, and then returns to the lower country. It is, however, certain, that tortoises can **subsist** even on those islands where there is no other water, than what falls during a few rainy days in the year.

---

methodically: in a very organised way
subsist: survive, exist

The inhabitants believe that these animals are absolutely deaf; certainly they do not overhear a person walking close behind them. I was always amused, when overtaking one of these great monsters as it was quietly pacing along, to see how suddenly, the instant I passed, it would draw in its head and legs, and uttering a deep hiss fall to the ground with a heavy sound, as if struck dead. I frequently got on their backs, and then, upon giving a few raps on the **hinder** part of the shell, they would rise up and walk away; but I found it very difficult to keep my balance.

The flesh of this animal is largely employed, both fresh and salted; and a beautifully clear oil is prepared from the fat. When a tortoise is caught, the man makes a slit in the skin near its tail, so as to see inside its body, whether the fat under the **dorsal** plate is thick. If it is not, the animal is **liberated**; and it is said to recover soon from this strange operation.

hinder: back, rear
dorsal: along the back
liberated: set free

The clash of ideas
Paul Strathern

Like most of the English people of his time, Darwin was a Christian, and accepted the Bible as the word of God. But he could no longer ignore the fact that the evidence he had collected simply did not fit the account given in the Bible, especially the first book, Genesis. This writer explains what Darwin's problem was.

According to the first book of Genesis: 'God created every living creature that moveth . . . every winged fowl . . . and every thing that creepeth on the face of the earth.' Each of these species had been specifically designed for the environment which it inhabited. This was known as the Argument from Design. Thus: fish had gills which enabled them to breathe under water, birds had wings, and creepy-crawlies were equipped with lots of wiggly things which enabled them to creep and crawl. Each species was **immutably** what it was, because it had been made that way in order to live the way it did. This not only answered all questions, but was the **Holy Writ**. To question it was to question God's wisdom.

But there always has to be someone who asks awkward questions – even if he makes sure he keeps them to himself. Darwin was now a respected member of the Victorian scientific community, and had no wish to be drummed out of the club for **blasphemy**. Fifty years before Robert Louis Stevenson wrote his classic story,

---

immutably: unchangeably
Holy Writ: sacred writings
blasphemy: insulting God

Darwin was already rehearsing the life of Dr Jekyll and Mr Hyde. In public the respectable Dr Jekyll remained every inch the Victorian gentleman. Meanwhile in secret Mr Hyde **imbibed** his heady potion of blasphemous ideas, tearing at the very foundations of all that was sacred.

According to the Argument from Design which followed on from **Creationism** members of a species living under similar circumstances should always resemble one another. (This was the environment for which they had been designed.) But Darwin had noticed that birds in the Galápagos Islands, and those of the same species living in the Cape Verde Islands, were in reality different – despite the fact that both groups of islands were virtually identical (remote, volcanic, tropical, etc.). In fact, the species living in the Cape Verde Islands were much closer to those found on the African mainland, whose environment was completely different. Was it possible that the birds on the Cape Verde Islands and those on the African mainland had **a common** ancestor? (Such a thing was quite impossible, according to the notion of **static** species held by the Creationists.)

Similarly, the finches on the different Galápagos Islands were each distinctly different – whereas according to Creationist theory they should have been identical, as they all shared the same environment. On the other hand there was the ostrich. In the pleasant climate of the Argentine pampas, Darwin had observed giant ostriches. Yet south in inhospitable Patagonia the ostriches were of a smaller species. Both of these closely resembled the African ostrich. According to Creationist theory, all these different ostriches had simply been created as separate

---

imbibed: drank down
Creationism: the belief that God created everything in six days
a common: the same
static: unchanging

species. But couldn't these different species be the result of the same original species developing and adapting itself to different circumstances in geographical isolation?

Under the influence of his heady potion, Mr Hyde was becoming convinced that **genesis** as described in the Bible was bunk.

---

genesis: the start of life

Activities

Darwin's life

1 This encyclopedia article is written for a young audience. It
is divided into two parts. The first is very brief, setting out
the key facts about Darwin. The second is a more detailed
account of his life, written like a biography. It is written in
the past tense and is organised chronologically using
temporal connectives. The greater part of the article
describes how Darwin came to develop his famous theory
'The Origin of Species.' Look carefully at the topic sentence
of each paragraph (the first sentence), which indicates what
the paragraph will be about. Use just the topic sentences in
this article to write an extension of the first part of the entry,
picking out the key facts about Darwin's life. You can use
sub-headings to group points if you wish.

2 Imagine that Darwin kept a diary during his childhood and
time spent as a student. Write an entry that expresses the
problems he encountered in trying to pursue his interest in
nature. Use the details from the article to help you but
remember to write in the first person and either the
present or the simple past tense.

Voyage of discovery

1 In this account of Darwin's voyage on HMS Beagle, the author
begins by writing from the point of view of the Argentinean
soldiers stationed at the local garrison in Bahia Blanca using
rhetorical questions. Why do you think he does this?

2 The author follows this with several paragraphs describing
Darwin's findings. Each paragraph approaches the subject
from a slightly different perspective. There is a description
of the place where Darwin found the fossilised bones of
prehistoric animals. Then there is an explanation of how
much people knew about palaeontology at the time. This
is followed by a description of the actual finding from

Darwin's viewpoint. After this is an explanation of what the find meant to Darwin. Following that there is a description of one animal in particular. Then comes an exploration of the link between the animals and the local vegetation. Next is an examination of what killed off the animals. Finally there is a description of the reaction of the ship's crew to Darwin's findings. Why do you think the author decided to structure the paragraphs of his account in this order? Can you suggest an alternative method of organising the material to create a different effect?

3 Write an entry in Darwin's journal for the evening after his discoveries at Bahia Blanca. Jot down the main finds and then end the entry with two or three of the main questions that are now bothering him.

The giant tortoise

1 Darwin wrote this account in 1839 and English has changed quite a lot since that time. Many of the expressions in his account are no longer used or would now be expressed in a different way.

Rewrite the following expressions as a modern writer might express them:

- 'Mr Lawson, an Englishman, who had at the time of our visit charge of the colony'
- 'some had afforded as much as 200 pounds of meat
- 'the larger islands alone possess springs
- 'at a considerable elevation'
- 'it was a curious spectacle to behold many of these great monsters'

2 Several companies give away key fact cards with their products, to encourage people to collect the cards and buy the product. The cards usually have a picture of the subject and a set of key facts about it. Create a key fact card for the giant tortoise: include data on its appearance, habitat, behaviour etc. Set out the information with clear headings. You might start off:

THE GIANT TORTOISE

Latin name: *Testudo indicus*

Found in: *the Galápagos Archipelago*

The clash of ideas

1 In order to show how difficult it was for Darwin's ideas to be accepted, the first paragraph of this account describes the views on creation at that time. It likens it to Holy Writ, which is decreed by God and therefore regarded as sacred and not to be questioned. Explain why this might be an effective device to illustrate Darwin's problem?

2 The author uses an analogy (comparison) in the second paragraph to show how Darwin had to lead two lives, appearing in public to believe what was acceptable to Victorian society and keeping his real opinions private. Identify with whom Darwin is compared, and explain why the author chooses to use this particular comparison.

3 Here are some extracts from Genesis which give an account of the creation of living things and the great flood. In pairs, pick out the parts of the account that you think Darwin was beginning to question.

CHAPTER 1
In the beginning God created the heaven and the earth . . .

And God said, Let the waters bring forth abundantly the moving creature that hath life, and fowl that may fly above the earth in the open firmament of heaven . . .

And God created great whales, and every living creature that moveth, which the waters brought forth abundantly, after their kind, and every winged fowl after his kind: and God saw that it was good . . .

And God said, Let the earth bring forth the living creature after his kind, cattle and creeping thing, and beast of the earth after his kind: and it was so . . .

And God said, Let us make man in our image, after our likeness . . .

CHAPTER 2
And on the seventh day God ended his work which he had made; and he rested on the seventh day from all his work which he had made.

CHAPTER 7
. . . And it came to pass after seven days, that the waters of the flood were upon the earth . . .

And all flesh died that moved upon the earth, both of fowl, and of cattle, and of beast, and of every creeping thing that creepeth upon the earth, and every man . . .

Comparing the extracts

1 Working in groups of six, take one text each and make notes on the following questions:

What are the main pieces of information given?

Does the extract seem to contain facts or opinions or both? (An example of a fact would be: 'Darwin embarked on the voyage in 1831.' But when Alan Moorehead writes 'it must have been about this time that he began to argue with Fitzroy . . .', that is his opinion.)

Who is writing or speaking? Whose point of view are we getting?

What would you say about the language? (Is it formal or informal? Is it aimed at a particular audience – if so, which?)

What tense is it in? (Present tense: 'The tortoise *is* very fond of water . . . '; or past tense: ' . . . Darwin *had observed* giant ostriches.'?)

Does this text have any key features that make it different from others? (For example, how can you tell that one of them is written for a younger audience?)

2 What have you learned – from all these texts taken together – about

(a) Charles Darwin's life and career; and

(b) his scientific discoveries and ideas? Look up the following sections to give you some ideas and then write an account of Charles Darwin for younger readers:

> *His life and career: Darwin's life; Voyage of discovery; The clash of ideas.*

> *His scientific discoveries and ideas: Darwin's life; Voyage of discovery; The giant tortoise; The clash of ideas.*

3 Pick another well-known figure from the world of science and technology. Then write two extracts from different types of biography on that person. For example, you might choose to write a few paragraphs from a biography, and a page from a school science textbook.

When you write your final drafts, leave a wide column down the side of the page. Then add notes in that column to show the differences between the two extracts that you have written.

ALSO IN

Heinemann
New Windmills

Founding Editors: Anne and Ian Serraillier

Chinua Achebe Things Fall Apart
David Almond Skellig
Maya Angelou I Know Why the Caged Bird Sings
Margaret Atwood The Handmaid's Tale
Jane Austen Pride and Prejudice
J G Ballard Empire of the Sun
Stan Barstow Joby; A Kind of Loving
Nina Bawden Carrie's War; Devil by the Sea; Kept in the Dark; The Finding; Humbug
Lesley Beake A Cageful of Butterflies
Malorie Blackman Tell Me No Lies; Words Last Forever
Ray Bradbury The Golden Apples of the Sun; The Illustrated Man
Betsy Byars The Midnight Fox; The Pinballs; The Not-Just-Anybody Family; The Eighteenth Emergency
Victor Canning The Runaways
Jane Leslie Conly Racso and the Rats of NIMH
Susan Cooper King of Shadows
Robert Cormier We All Fall Down; Heroes
Roald Dahl Danny, The Champion of the World; The Wonderful Story of Henry Sugar; George's Marvellous Medicine; The BFG; The Witches; Boy; Going Solo; Matilda; My Year
Anita Desai The Village by the Sea
Charles Dickens A Christmas Carol; Great Expectations; Hard Times; Oliver Twist; A Charles Dickens Selection
Berlie Doherty Granny was a Buffer Girl; Street Child
Roddy Doyle Paddy Clarke Ha Ha Ha
Anne Fine The Granny Project
Jamila Gavin The Wheel of Surya
Graham Greene The Third Man and The Fallen Idol; Brighton Rock
Thomas Hardy The Withered Arm and Other Wessex Tales
L P Hartley The Go-Between
Ernest Hemmingway The Old Man and the Sea; A Farewell to Arms
Barry Hines A Kestrel For A Knave
Nigel Hinton Getting Free; Buddy; Buddy's Song; Out of the Darkness
Anne Holm I Am David
Janni Howker Badger on the Barge; The Nature of the Beast; Martin Farrell

Pete Johnson The Protectors
Jennifer Johnston Shadows on Our Skin
Geraldine Kaye Comfort Herself
Daniel Keyes Flowers for Algernon
Dick King-Smith The Sheep-Pig
Elizabeth Laird Red Sky in the Morning; Kiss the Dust
D H Lawrence The Fox and The Virgin and the Gypsy; Selected Tales
George Layton The Swap
Harper Lee To Kill a Mockingbird
C Day Lewis The Otterbury Incident
Joan Lingard Across the Barricades; The File on Fraulein Berg
Penelope Lively The Ghost of Thomas Kempe
Jack London The Call of the Wild; White Fang
Bernard MacLaverty Cal; The Best of Bernard Mac Laverty
James Vance Marshall Walkabout
Ian McEwan The Daydreamer; A Child in Time
Michael Morpurgo My Friend Walter; The Wreck of the Zanzibar;
The War of Jenkins' Ear; Why the Whales Came; Arthur, High King
of Britain; Kensuke's Kingdom; Hereabout Hill
Beverley Naidoo No Turning Back
Bill Naughton The Goalkeeper's Revenge
New Windmill A Charles Dickens Selection
New Windmill Book of Classic Short Stories
New Windmill Book of Fiction and Non-fiction: Taking Off!
New Windmill Book of Haunting Tales
New Windmill Book of Humorous Stories: Don't Make Me Laugh
New Windmill Book of Nineteenth Century Short Stories
New Windmill Book of Non-fiction: Get Real!
New Windmill Book of Non-fiction: Real Lives, Real Times
New Windmill Book of Scottish Short Stories
New Windmill Book of Short Stories: Fast and Curious
New Windmill Book of Short Stories: From Beginning to End
New Windmill Book of Short Stories: Into the Unknown
New Windmill Book of Short Stories: Tales with a Twist
New Windmill Book of Short Stories: Trouble in Two Centuries
New Windmill Book of Short Stories: Ways with Words
New Windmill Book of Short Stories by Women
New Windmill Book of Stories from many Cultures and Traditions:
Fifty-Fifty Tutti-Frutti Chocolate-Chip
New Windmill Book of Stories from Many Genres: Myths, Murders
and Mysteries

How many have you read?